Effective Meetings

A Practical Guide

BRUCE PARTRIDGE

FriesenPress

Suite 300 - 990 Fort St
Victoria, BC, V8V 3K2
Canada

www.friesenpress.com

Copyright © 2016 by Bruce Partridge

First Edition — 2016

All rights reserved.

No part of this publication may be reproduced in any form, or by any means, electronic or mechanical, including photocopying, recording, or any information browsing, storage, or retrieval system, without permission in writing from FriesenPress.

Library and Archives Canada Cataloguing in Publication

Partridge, Bruce J., author
Effective meetings : a practical guide / Bruce Partridge.

Issued in print and electronic formats.
ISBN 978-1-4602-8837-5 (hardback).
ISBN 978-1-4602-8838-2 (paperback).
ISBN 978-1-4602-8839-9 (pdf)

1. Meetings--Handbooks, manuals, etc. I. Title.
AS6.P375 2016
060.4'2
C2016-904451-3
C2016-904452-1

ISBN
978-1-4602-8837-5 (Hardcover)
978-1-4602-8838-2 (Paperback)
978-1-4602-8839-9 (eBook)

1. BUSINESS & ECONOMICS, BUSINESS COMMUNICATION, MEETINGS & PRESENTATIONS

Distributed to the trade by The Ingram Book Company

Contents

About this Book

This book had its roots several decades ago when I was an undergraduate. A faculty member at Oberlin College, Dr. J. Jeffrey Auer, was recognized as an authority on meeting procedures and had written a small book on the subject. Having observed my struggles as I chaired several large student meetings, he took pity on me. He gave me some much-needed advice on how to prepare for and to chair a meeting.

When I tried some of his suggestions I was astonished to discover how much easier life was for me and for those attending the meetings. For the first time I realized that there is both an art and a science to chairing a meeting. And I resolved to learn more about this fascinating subject. I have been learning about it since that day.

Throughout my life each of my several career paths has required me to attend or to chair meeting after meeting. As a research physicist I met almost daily with other researchers from our lab to share ideas and findings. In my next career as a university administrator, then a university vice president, and finally a university president, every weekday my calendar had at least one, if not three, meetings with faculty members, or with administrators and managers, or with members of the public. In my next career as a lawyer and then general counsel and corporate secretary of a multi-national corporation, and still later as manager of a large law office in Hong Kong, my day was less crowded and yet there were still three or four meetings a week. On top of these meetings there were boards of churches, strata councils (the Canadian equivalent of U.S. home owners' associations), and various volunteer organizations such as youth recreation commissions, community theatres, and groups that support the mentally challenged. These organizations share one common factor – their success depends on effective meetings.

Over many years, in three different countries, I have tried a wide variety of approaches and different techniques and methods. The outcomes have also varied – some of my experiments have succeeded beyond expectations; others have been total busts!

Now it seems right to share with you the principles and simple methods that I have found actually *worked* – worked in the sense of helping to shape meetings so they can be effective, efficient, and pleasant, and in allowing everyone to take a direct hand in the process. The result is *Effective Meetings.*

Before I outline the book's contents, let me make clear what it is NOT about.

There are many books and articles that attempt to clarify and explain *Robert's Rules of Order* or other similar books on parliamentary procedure. These publications serve an important purpose. But while this book does not conflict with *Robert's*, it approaches meetings from a different standpoint. It is not a book of rules; it is a guide that sets out in simple terms what you, as the chair of a meeting, can do before, during, and after it to make it more democratic and more effective as well as more efficient.

The simple, practical steps described will help you to enlist the support of other members, encourage them to suggest fresh ideas, and help lead them to making informed decisions. Thoughtfully designing the agenda, keeping discussion focused, and allocating times will keep meetings productive and allow participants to complete their work within a reasonable time.

Simplified approaches to minute-taking help to ensure that the record includes what is important and omits what is of little importance. Then, an easy method of archiving decisions will make sure that policies are continually updated and kept available instead of being effectively forgotten and lost almost as soon as they have been approved.

To keep it simple, *Effective Meetings* is written from the standpoint of the chair (or president or convener, or whatever the title might be) of the board of a community, religious, or other volunteer organization. But identical principles apply and can be easily adapted to professional, union, political and, in fact, all other types of meetings in which a group is expected to meet, discuss, and make decisions about topics that are important for an organization.

In its structure this book follows the flow from the first moment in which you start thinking about a meeting, through preparing for it, leading, and conducting it, to following up and keeping a usable record of its decisions.

Chapter 1 describes and explains what it is that makes a meeting successful. It also discusses what constitutes organizational culture and how you can work within it to permit a transformation to new and better methods. Chapter 2 is devoted to the chair's relationships to the other participants and to the special roles of the chair in facilitating, managing, and mentoring.

The next six chapters are centered on what you can do during the meeting itself. Chapters 3 and 4 cover the principles and practices by which the agenda shapes the meeting through its organization of topics, choice of wording, and allocation of time.

Chapters 5 through 7 set out advance preparation for the meeting, opening it, shaping discussion of its major topics, and closing it. Chapter 8 suggests ways to deal with some of the more challenging situations that are likely to pop up from time to time.

Chapter 9 describes how minutes can be most useful to the board and to the larger organization. It also introduces a simple system through which decisions, once made, are recorded and made available for future reference instead of being buried in many pages of descriptions of meetings that will have almost no interest for anyone in the future.

Throughout, I have described incidents that illustrate points in the text. To protect privacy, I have changed the names and in some cases also the kind of organization involved. Of course, the words quoted may not be exactly what was said, but I have reflected the intent as best I can. In all other respects, the incidents took place exactly as they appear here.

The book wraps up with four short appendices. They provide the reader with direction to:

A) Develop practical codes of conduct;

B) Use a simplified guide to parliamentary procedures;

C) Make financial reports understandable; and

D) Find the right words to use.

Chapter 1

The Secrets of Successful Meetings

Sometimes life seems to revolve around meetings. Whether we are on the job or in the community, meetings are a part of the daily or weekly round. We attend them because our organizations have purposes we believe in, whether those organizations be volunteer or professional, whether they are religious, political or charitable. We attend meetings to manage businesses, civic affairs, and a whole host of other common, shared purposes. Through meetings, we participate in the life of our communities.

And since meetings are so important to what we do and how we do it, we may well ask how effective these meetings are. Can they can be improved? Often, the answer is yes.

If your answer is yes, this book will help you design better meetings. And through such design, help you work with others more effectively to accomplish your organization's purpose.

Designing a successful meeting

Many of us find that meetings can be described in one of two ways: those that are enjoyable, relatively short, and get something done, and those that are boring, waste time, and accomplish very little.

Successful meetings don't just happen. They are the result of thoughtful and careful planning and action by someone who knows the characteristics that distinguish a truly successful meeting from the great majority of meetings.

Designing a successful meeting, an effective meeting, is both an art and a science. It requires specialized knowledge and skill. Knowledge you can gain from this book; skill you can acquire through day-by-day experience. However, what you will need to create successful meetings is relatively easy to acquire. Just by picking up this book you have started on a fast learning curve.

Meeting for a purpose

But we need an immediate reason to commit time to meetings. Usually that reason is simple. The organization in which we are participating needs to make decisions. And decisions made collaboratively by the interested members of a group are likely to be better than independent decisions made by just one person.

Is this confidence in meetings justified? Sometimes yes; sometimes no. The difference lies in whether they do or do not result in decisions that advance the purposes of the organization. A meeting can best achieve this positive result if it has certain characteristics.

These characteristics may be summarized in six key elements. They are:

- The meeting is focused on and results in useful decisions;
- Its decisions are based on accurate and timely information;
- Participants have equal opportunities to take part;
- Participants treat each other with dignity and respect;
- Its decisions are recorded in ways that make them available to those people who need to know of them; and
- The results are worth the time and effort devoted before, during, and after the meeting.

Meeting these objectives may seem a formidable challenge, but the rest of this book will show how as chair you can use simple, practical methods that will painlessly provide all of them to meetings.

For now, we will expand on and describe more fully each of these characteristics.

Focus on purpose

The first characteristic of a successful meeting is that it is fully focused on the purposes for which it has been called. During the meeting the participants devote most of their time and energy to discussing the selected topics and making decisions about them. The advance planning, the conduct of the meeting, and the follow-up afterwards – everything is directed to this underlying theme of effective decision-making.

One measure you can test is when an agenda topic is up for discussion, to observe whether everything that is said is directly related to it or whether there is a lot of unrelated conversation. A meeting can quickly go off the rails if discussion wanders away from the current topic, or if too much time is being spent on routine matters that don't really require discussion.

For the meeting to be a success the chair has to recognize these and other indicators of misdirection so that action can be taken to return the meeting to its important business.

Availability of information

The second essential characteristic is closely intertwined with the first. It is that whatever decisions are made are *informed* decisions – that is that the participants have had the information they needed to understand the situation, to have evaluated it seriously, and to have reached conclusions as to what to do about it. How often have you heard someone say, "The board members made a dumb decision because they didn't know that..." or "...because they forgot that..."?

Having the relevant information does not guarantee that the participants will make the best possible decisions, but they certainly cannot do so if they don't have that information.

Good decisions require everyone to be operating from the same set of facts. It can't be assumed that all of the participants are equally well informed about every topic that is to be discussed. All of the participants may be somewhat familiar with a topic. But usually one participant knows some facts, while others know other facts, and no one knows all of the relevant facts. Consequently, each participant will be coming to the discussion with a slightly different understanding. Unless care is taken to provide everyone with the same information, there will be confusion and misunderstanding. At best, precious meeting time will need to be spent getting everyone onto the same page to start.

Some ways in which to provide these equal starting points are discussed in the following chapters, especially in Chapter 5.

Active participation

For the meeting to function effectively, all of the participants must have had the opportunity to take an active part in the meeting. It is not a coincidence that the term "participant" is often used throughout this book to refer to the members of the group that you are planning to chair.

A participant is someone who takes an active part in the events in question. During a meeting you may observe that a few members are not actively *participating.* Often this is because a few other participants have monopolized the discussion. Then the silent ones' ideas, knowledge, and judgment are lost to the group. It can almost be as if they weren't there at all. To avoid this waste, the meeting must be conducted so that ideas and suggestions are equally welcomed and encouraged from all members of the group. Ways of encouraging widespread participation are spelled out in Chapters 5 through 7.

Participants who feel that all have equal rights and responsibilities in the meeting also feel more committed to its work. A sense of ownership is intangible but powerful. With this sense of ownership, the active participants take responsibility for helping the meeting to progress, instead of leaving its management to the person who is presiding. If the discussion is wandering, if one member is dominating, if others seem withdrawn, or if tensions are building up, necessary corrective action may be taken by any participant as well as by the chair. This sharing of responsibility relieves the chair from having to be a constant disciplinarian, which over time would tend to antagonize the participants and erode the chair's effectiveness.

For example, Chapter 5 describes how you can offer the participants an opportunity to make suggestions about what items will be discussed at the upcoming meeting. They may seldom take advantage of the opportunity, but the fact that you made it possible will counteract any tendency for them to think that you and/or a small inner circle, are running the meeting for your own ends.

Mutual respect

A meeting can progress most comfortably and effectively if its atmosphere is one of collaboration – one in which the participants feel they are working pleasantly together to achieve common goals.

For this sense of collaboration, the participants must feel, and show, respect for each other and for each other's opinions. This is more than common courtesy. It involves actively listening to what others say, allowing them to finish without being interrupted, and keeping the discussion pointed to the issues at hand and not to the personalities of the participants.

Many organizations have found that adopting a Code of Conduct can help remind meeting participants of how they should be relating to each other during meetings.

A CODE OF CONDUCT TO THE RESCUE

A number of years ago, I was appointed chair of a commission on higher education. The commission consisted of about sixteen university presidents, most of them considerably senior to me in age and experience. I was only a vice president. I approached the first meeting feeling quite insecure.

At the first meeting, I proposed that the members begin by developing a Code of Conduct. One influential member, Ted, grumbled, "We have serious work to do. Let's not waste time on this touchy-feely nonsense."

I persisted and the group - probably to placate me - agreed to create and approve a short written code. It didn't take long since, because of their work, everyone in the group had had prior experience with such codes. The draft covered such matters as not interrupting a speaker, keeping language temperate, and not questioning others' motives. It was brief and didn't address some of the issues that I had had in mind, but it seemed as good as we might get in the circumstances.

Nothing further was said about the Code of Conduct. Two or three meetings later, the discussion became rather heated. One member, Phil, lost his temper and sputtered, "Tom, you're being a damned fool." Before I could say anything, Ted (the skeptic who had opposed "wasting time" on a Code of Conduct) interrupted with "Hold on, Phil. Remember our Code of Conduct. Tom may *be* a damned fool, but we agreed not to tell him so."

Everyone, including Phil and Tom, laughed. Phil said, "Sorry, Tom." The meeting cooled down and proceeded smoothly and pleasantly from then on.

Appendix A offers some suggestions as to how you can work with the participants to develop a Code of Conduct and a few of the items you might hope will be included in it.

Access to a record of decisions

Most groups keep minutes of their meetings. Minutes can be a jumble of useless information, or alternatively, a crisp and clear record of decisions and other important matters. Chapter 9 describes in detail what should go into minutes, what should be left out, and how to present the relevant material.

Keeping the record of the meeting is only a part of the task. The same chapter describes ways in which the minutes can be a valuable resource for the board and the organization in the future, instead of being written and then promptly forgotten. In particular, Chapter 9 describes innovative methods that make it easy and convenient for anyone in the future to find relevant information.

Optimum time and effort

A meeting necessarily requires the participants to commit considerable time and effort. For them to want to continue to make this commitment, they must have reason to believe that the meeting is the best use that they can make of these two precious commodities.

TIME WELL SPENT?

My friend Wendy chairs the board of a strata council (the Canadian equivalent of a home owners' association in the U.S.) that controls the townhouse she owns. She told me that most of one monthly meeting was taken up with the question of whether to purchase a new vacuum cleaner (to be used in the common areas), and if so, which model and attachments to choose.

This topic occupied the meeting. It crowded out any discussion of the organization's serious financial problems – problems that, despite Wendy's efforts, the board members were apparently unprepared or unwilling to face and discuss.

As might be expected from this example, this particular board was noted for its long, unproductive meetings. It seldom produced any innovative ideas or programs, and it barely kept up with the minor problems that continually arose from daily operations.

It was only after the election of entirely new members and a conscious re-ordering of priorities that the reconstituted board began to address and fix the organization's financial problems.

Many boards follow a similar pattern of allowing their time and energies to be frittered away on small, simple items while ducking the more difficult issues. Correcting this tendency can begin with the selection of topics for the agenda, a subject that will be covered in Chapter 3.

We know that one of the most common complaints about meetings is that they are too long. There are limits on how long anyone can concentrate on the business of a meeting. If the meeting is allowed to continue beyond that time, minds wander, concentration is lost, and little is likely to be accomplished. What little is done is likely not to be the best.

If too much meeting time is spent on one topic, the other topics are cut short. Or, to get through its essential business, the meeting has to drag on long past the time when the participants' attention has drifted away. So, precious meeting time must be rationed. This rationing must be done in ways that are accepted and supported by the participants who will be affected by it.

To make possible this rationing of time, methods must also be put into place that promptly dispose of routine matters and those that are noncontroversial or of little importance. This means having to wean the group from a common human tendency. This tendency is for a group to spend time and energy on small, insignificant matters that are easy to resolve, to the exclusion of more important, larger matters that require careful thought, hard work, and yes, the risk that a decision might prove to have been wrong. Using other methods found in Chapters 4 through 8 will conserve enough time to allow full and open discussion of the main topics, while keeping the total meeting within reasonable time limits.

All six of the essential meeting characteristics are, in various ways, reflections of the organizational culture, which is the subject of the next section.

Identifying the organization's culture

Every organization has an organizational culture that determines how its members are expected to act in various circumstances. These expectations do not appear in written form, but they govern individual assumptions and reactions even more strongly than would a set of written rules.

Within the organization, its culture is usually taken for granted. It is not talked about and most people are only vaguely aware that it exists. Unseen as it may be, though, the organizational culture determines the extent to which the organization functions democratically or autocratically. In fact, it underlies and shapes everything that happens within the organization.

The organization's culture governs and is revealed by such factors as how members react to uncertainty, how money is or is not discussed, and how newcomers are or are not welcomed and integrated into the organization. It even seems to dictate how people dress for meetings, whether they arrive on time or drift in late, and how they greet each other as they arrive at a meeting or even when they meet on the street.

Since you are reading this book you probably have in mind improving some of the practices and attitudes of the group that you will chair. Your success in doing so will be greatly influenced by your understanding of and your ability to deal with two aspects of organizational culture that will become apparent as you introduce new methods.

One is how people react to *innovations.* The other is how they deal with *differences of opinion*. We'll look at each in detail.

Discerning culture's influence on innovation

Let's start with what you can expect within the organizational culture as you propose new ideas and new methods. It is natural for everyone to feel some hesitancy. After all, it is easier for us all to continue doing what we have been doing, than to learn to do something different.

Besides, if things are done differently than they have been in the past, the outcomes will also be different and unpredictable, and we all are (wisely) a bit uneasy about the unknown.

If the culture is one of comparative openness, however, a bit of experimentation with new practices will be accepted and if properly presented, actively supported.

On the other hand, if the organizational culture is closed and rigid, any variation from past practice may be seen as disruptive. The prevailing attitude is that everything is perfect as it is and should not be disturbed. Innovation is frowned upon if not actively feared. It occurs so infrequently that the organization's leaders have seldom had to adapt to anything new and are likely to feel threatened by the need to do so.

In this case you will find that reform requires laying more solid groundwork and takes longer. But don't despair. It can be done!

The question then arises: How can you tell which is the kind of culture you will be facing, and from this, how you can best deal with it? The best gauge can be found from observing the day-to-day activities within the organization. Then see where they fit within the chart that follows.

Clues to an organization's culture		
ORGANIZATIONAL FEATURE	OPEN TO INNOVATION	RESISTANT TO INNOVATION
Membership on the governing board and on important committees	At least one or two *new* members are elected to office every year (or two years if they serve two-year terms).	Membership circulates among a small inner circle; an officer position is typically held by the same person for several years.

Board agendas	Largely devoted to specific questions and problems; agenda topics are quite different from meeting to meeting.	Agendas look much the same from meeting to meeting and are heavily dependent on reports of past activities.
Attendance at meetings of the board and of committees.	Usually, all members attend; when they cannot, they advise the chair in advance.	At many meetings at least two or three members are absent, often without having warned the chair.
Decisions made	Most decisions determine specific actions on behalf of the organization; periodically some shape the long-range future of the organization.	Most decisions relate to minor operating matters; little attention is paid to the overall condition of, or the future of, the organization.
Written operating policies	Discussed at many board meetings; intentionally amended from time to time as new situations arise.	Little discussion of policies, because "everyone knows what to do."
Financial reports	Summaries are provided to board members at least monthly; comparisons are frequently made with annual and five-year projections.	Board members make little effort to understand and analyze financial reports, leaving detailed consideration of them largely to the treasurer.

If you observe that the clues fall mostly into the middle column, you have the good fortune to be operating within a relatively open organizational culture. In such a culture you will probably be able to proceed with your plans with little opposition, and with positive support from those affected.

Conversely, if your observations tend to fall in the third column, it probably means that the organization is hobbled with a rigid culture. In this case, at first it will be extremely difficult to reshape the culture of the organization directly. But a board or committee is much smaller and consequently more malleable. As you succeed in reforming the culture within the smaller group, its newfound insights will gradually seep out into the parent organization and have a positive effect there as well.

Whatever the culture may be, you will need to proceed carefully to avoid backlash. You will have to explain your plans thoroughly, in terms of how they will affect individuals. And, of course, the emphasis of your explanations will be on how the innovations will provide advantages for the people involved. The next chapter spells out some of the techniques you can use to help orient new members and to re-orient current members of the group.

In the process, it may soften any hesitation to the introduction of new methods if you suggest that they be tried for six months or so and that at the end of that trial period, any further refinement could be considered. When the new methods have been functioning for this trial period, they should have shown enough improvement over the former practices that they will have earned general acceptance. Then only minor tweaking will be needed, while the overall framework will remain intact.

De-emphasizing "change"

As has been pointed out, even in the most open of organizational cultures there will be some natural resistance to change. A wise person has said, "We all welcome change, as long as it happens to someone else."

We shouldn't be surprised that some people will be a bit reluctant to adopt new concepts and new methods. After all, everyone may be more comfortable with continuing to do "what we have always done," than to do something different. And there is also the unspoken fear that we will be criticized if we move away from familiar paths.

"What if we don't change anything at all ... and something magical just happens."

To counteract this natural hesitancy you will want to de-emphasize *change*. You can do this to some extent by your choice of words. Throughout all of the transition period you do not speak of, or even think of, making a *change*. Instead, you will be proposing *to do things a little differently*; you will be suggesting *modifications* and *innovations* in methods and procedures; you will be *introducing new concepts*. But you will NEVER think of or say that scary word *ch..ge.*

This may seem silly and a trivial point. But word choice has power, and its symbolism has a greater impact on our attitudes than we are likely to realize. Just saying (or thinking) the word can raise all of the fears that work against acceptance of improvement.

Thinking of new ways brings us to the question of how a meeting functions. In particular, let's look at the second aspect of organizational culture that may be especially relevant to the need to improve meetings. This is how the organization deals with differences of opinion.

Welcoming disagreement

An organizational culture that predisposes its members to resist reform is almost invariably accompanied by a widespread fear of disagreement of any kind. After an opinion has been expressed, it is felt to be rude or even disruptive for anyone to express a differing opinion.

Yet, the usual reason for holding a meeting is to make decisions. Good decisions are most likely to arise from the exchange of ideas. It is only if participants have different views, that is, *disagreement,* that there is any point in having a meeting to discuss a topic.

This comes down to saying bluntly that the *reason for having a meeting is to encourage disagreement*!

It follows that a successful meeting is one in which the chair and the participants are not only comfortable with disagreement, but actually expect and welcome it. They take it, rightly, as a healthy part of the process of arriving at a decision.

An underlying fear of disagreement leads to members proudly repeating the myth that the organization is "one big happy family." Where this myth prevails, it is almost certain that the organization not only lacks new ideas and projects, but is firmly committed to enforcing existing practices and habits.

Some members may find it comforting and reassuring that everyone seems to always agree about everything. Unfortunately, this bland uniformity often comes from silence – the silence of those who have different opinions but hesitate to express them because they don't want to be classified as trouble-makers.

As a result of this self-imposed silence, everyone just goes along with the crowd. There is no meaningful discussion and the organization muddles along month after month, year after year, with few fresh ideas or activities.

From time to time small problems arise in every organization. It is a well-known phenomenon that when small problems are not addressed while they are still small, some of them will remain buried beneath the surface until they fester enough to break out into serious conflict – which is likely to happen periodically in such circumstances.

The following true story illustrates one outcome when this toxic but unacknowledged form of organizational culture exists – that is, when it makes up an underlying characteristic of the prevailing organizational culture.

A DESTRUCTIVE ORGANIZATIONAL CULTURE

Several years ago I was asked to chair a meeting of a community organization that was facing the question of whether to take on a particular project. This project would consume most of the organization's volunteer time and a sizable chunk of its funds. After several months of fact-finding and deliberation it had come time to make a final decision – to go ahead or to drop the project.

At the general meeting at which the decision was to be made, an unprecedented 90 of the organization's 112 members attended, indicating the high degree of the members' interest.

I knew that the organization had a culture in which if someone expressed an opinion and anyone disagreed, it was seen as almost a personal attack on the original speaker. Disagreement was definitely NOT welcomed. Consequently, I in chairing the meeting, I was especially determined to keep the door open for any dissent. I happened to know personally some of the members who ardently supported the project, as well as some others who just as strongly opposed it. To keep the meeting fair and balanced I planned to alternate recognition between pro and con speakers.

This turned out to be difficult, however, because after the first speaker had passionately supported the project and the second speaker had mildly opposed it, all remaining speakers expressed their support. There were no further speakers who opposed the project. I was puzzled because I knew that a sizable contingent of members didn't want the organization to go ahead with it but they weren't speaking up.

I finally called for the vote. The organization's bylaws required that approval of this kind of important motion be by a two-thirds affirmative vote. I had the members stand to vote. I had appointed two tellers to make the count. They reported 51 votes for the project. I then asked for those opposed and only three members stood up. Of course, I declared the motion approved by 51 to 3, which more than met the required two-thirds vote.

After the meeting several members quit the organization in anger at the organization's decision. I asked one couple who were resigning why, if they so strongly opposed the motion, they had not voted against it. They said: "So many members had voted for the motion, there wasn't any point in voting against it *and looking bad.*"

I pointed out to them that 36 of the members present hadn't voted one way or the other. If 23 of those who hadn't cast a vote at all had stood up to vote against the project, it would have made the vote 51 to 26. This would have been less than the required two-thirds vote and the project would have been rejected.

Afterward, I reflected on what I might have done, as chair, to overcome the cultural blockage that prevented those people from voting for what they believed and thus changing the outcome. Reluctantly, I concluded that the organizational culture of avoiding disagreement was apparently too powerful to be overcome in a single meeting.

Keeping disagreement from becoming conflict

So, we can say: "Disagreement is good." At the same time, we recognize that "Conflict is bad."

The two are completely different. When disagreement turns into conflict it often stems from having confused the two, despite their differences from each other.

Disagreement is the holding of *differing opinions*. *Conflict* involves *animosity or hostility between people*. Disagreement relates to *issues*; conflict relates to *persons*.

There is a crucial difference between how disagreement and conflict are experienced during a meeting. In disagreeing about an issue, participants can listen to each other as they work together to find the best solutions. In a conflict, on the other hand, those who are involved lose sight of the issues and concentrate instead on attempting to win points. If a meeting has winners and losers, everyone loses.

How can you, as chair, help to keep disagreement from slipping into conflict?

The key ingredient in preventing this deterioration is mutual respect. As long as participants respect each other they can disagree on major issues and still relate positively to the other participants. That is disagreement without conflict.

How is this quality of mutual respect reflected? Its most obvious indication is in the ways that participants react when others are speaking. At the most elemental level, a negative indicator is if participants interrupt each other without waiting for people to finish saying what they have in mind. The positive measure, on the other hand, is when participants actively listen to what is being said instead of just going on with their own thoughts and ideas as if others have not said anything meaningful.

From your vantage point as chair you ask yourself, "When two participants disagree on a point, do they stick to the issues or do they slip into personal attacks, either directly or by implication?"

Many of the suggestions in this and later chapters are about ways that you, as a pro-active leader-manager, can make sure that the meetings benefit from disagreement while containing it so that it does not turn into conflict. For the longer term, as chair you can help re-direct the culture within the board toward greater comfort with disagreement. And you can hope that this more positive attitude will quietly and unobtrusively reshape the parent organization as well.

Defusing conflict

In an organization and especially in a small group such as a board or committee, a minor personal tension, if not corrected at an early stage, can escalate into more widespread conflict. Damage to the organization or the group can be best prevented if, before such a situation has arisen, the organization has established a procedure to be followed and at the first indications of serious interpersonal conflict, steps are taken to ease the tensions.

Some organizations have established a policy that when conflict appears on the horizon, in order to continue in membership, each member involved must be willing to take part in the organization's established conflict-resolution procedure.

Usually, the prescribed procedure is for a specifically named officer to meet privately with the two antagonists. Because the officer is seldom a professional counselor, the intention at this stage is not to mediate in a formal sense. Instead, the arrangement is designed to provide an opportunity for each of the two antagonists to express their concerns and to listen to the other's concerns.

Often this is a long step toward resolving the conflict. When two warring individuals actually listen to each other they often find that their differences are not as serious as they had thought.

If this informal session does not resolve the situation, the organization may decide that the conflict is sufficiently damaging to the organization to make it worthwhile to engage the services of a professional mediator. The organization should bear the cost of this mediation. Otherwise, there might be an unfair disparity between the antagonists' respective abilities to cover the cost.

If mediation is not successful, it may be necessary to consider instituting proceedings to expel one or both antagonists. Conflict seldom escalates to this level, but in the rare instance when it does, it requires considerable caution and tact.

All too often such a situation leads to formal legal action. In such an event, special complications often arise because of things that have been said or done before seeking legal advice. So, if the situation seems to be headed in this direction, *run, don't walk* to a law firm that specializes in employment law.

Distinguishing discussion from debate

You may have seen books on parliamentary procedure and even some on the conduct of meetings that use the term "debate" to refer to an exchange of ideas. Here and throughout this book, the term used is "discussion."

This is more than a simple choice of words. The difference is in how the participants think and act – whether they are debating or discussing.

Let's look for a moment at how a debate functions. Each debater comes to the debate prepared to express one particular opinion and to show that the opposing debaters are wrong. Debaters don't expect those on the other side to change their minds. Each debater just tries to show that an opposing view is misguided and should be disregarded.

At the end of the debate, the debaters all still defend the positions with which they started. No debater has changed position in the slightest.

When a debate is over, an outside judge decides who has been the most persuasive, rather than who has the best solution to the question that was posed.

Finally, in a debate there is a *winner* and a *loser*.

All of these aspects of a debate are the exact opposite of the qualities of a successful meeting. You do not want the participants to latch onto a fixed position; you want them to listen to opposing views and to think about them. Instead of participants having to choose sides, you hope they will present several different points of view that will blend together. You want them to keep open minds and be willing to change their original position if they are convinced this would be an improvement. No one tries to show that others are wrong. Finally, the success of the discussion is measured by the effectiveness of the decision and not by who was the most persuasive. The outcome is not decided by an outside judge; it comes from the group reaching agreement, which, while perhaps not perfect, is the best they can collectively reach.

Finally, and most important, there will be no winners and no losers – all share positively in the outcome.

Recognizing these differences in meaning between the two terms; this book is not about "debate," it is about "discussion."

As chair, one of your key objectives is to do everything possible to keep discussion from slipping into becoming a debate. You may find it useful to use the more accurate term, "discussion" (and not "debate"), when talking – and yes, when thinking – about a meeting.

This responsibility and much else falls on the shoulders of the chair, whose role is taken up in the next chapter.

Chapter 2

The Successful Chair

What part does the chair play in the creation of outstanding meetings?

For the purposes of this book, a meeting's chair can be any person who presides at a meeting, regardless of whether that officer is called the president, moderator, coordinator, chairperson, convener, or some other title.

When people think about what a chair does, one common image is of someone who takes the most dominant role in the meeting, expressing strong opinions on every topic and driving the meeting to conclusions that he or she has largely decided upon in advance.

This is one way to function while presiding at a meeting. But if the chair is to have made the decisions, and the others who attend are there only to endorse the chair's decisions, why bother to have a meeting?

There is a better way to serve as chair – one that gets the best from the participants. It allows the ideas and opinions of all of the participants to be welcomed and decisions to be made in collaboration. The suggestions in this book are designed to help tap this collective mind power and to bring about the most effective decisions, as well as the most productive and enjoyable meetings.

Furthermore, presiding at a meeting is only one of many related tasks that fall to the chair. The ways in which these other tasks are performed determine, to a large extent, how successful the chair will be in conducting the meeting.

The role of the chair, as set out in this book, differs from the traditional role of a semi-dictator who almost forces the group to whatever decision the chair has already chosen. Here the chair *assists* the other participants to pool their opinions, experience, and understanding so *they*, in combination with but not dominated by the chair, arrive at the best possible decisions.

Facilitating, managing, and mentoring

For a meeting to be an unqualified success, the chair performs three different kinds of tasks: *Facilitating, Managing,* and *Mentoring.* The three are closely interrelated, but they are different and require different approaches and different skills.

One definition of facilitate is: "*To make (an action, result, etc.) easier, less difficult, more easily achieved.*"

The *facilitator* role is aimed at *efficiency* – getting things done quickly, thoroughly, and completely with the least possible fuss and confusion.

As facilitator, the chair makes sure that physical arrangements are made for the meeting to be conducted comfortably and without interruption. The facilitator arranges for complete and timely paper flow; ensures that all participants understand what is happening during the meeting; and sees that decisions are appropriately recorded and made known to those who need to know of them. The facilitator serves to keep the business of the meeting orderly and its progress fair to everyone.

The chair, as *manager*, looks to efficiency as well, but the primary focus is on *effectiveness* – arriving at the best possible decisions and means of implementing them.

When acting as manager you monitor the progress of business within the meeting so that all participants are able to contribute to the best of their individual and collective abilities. As manager you help to keep discussion focused on the issues to be decided, so that time allotments are observed. You help to shape proceedings so that goals are met, and participants operate collaboratively and for a common purpose.

As *mentor,* you introduce the participants to new practices and policies that make possible the facilitation and management that underlie the other aspects of the meetings. During discussions in meetings you are ready to suggest how the participants might find common ground for a decision that is developing and then how they can sharpen their focus in formulating it. You serve as a positive role model for the participants and others, providing guidance when appropriate but without dictating.

The mentoring function is often less direct than the other two functions. It includes demonstrating and explaining the proposed methods in ways that make sense to the participants.

You have vital and far-reaching responsibilities as both facilitator and as manager. These roles are the most visible as you prepare for, organize, and chair the meetings and follow up after them. But it is as a mentor that you will have the greatest overall effect, not just within the board but also throughout the whole organization.

These three roles are challenging. Do they mean that to fulfill them you must be a miracle worker? Not at all. Instead, the concepts and methods in the following chapters will arm you with all that you will need to be a super-successful chair as you prepare for a meeting, conduct it, and follow up after it.

Serving as an example

Whether you intend it or not, how you act personally will have an influence on how the other participants act. This is, of course, true about everyone, but it is especially true about the chair.

People are very sensitive to moods. If you are cheerful and upbeat when you come to a meeting this will set the tone for the meeting. If throughout the meeting you remain cool and unflappable, this will go a long way toward keeping a heated discussion from becoming argumentative. If the chair has a consistently calm attitude, this allows a meeting to proceed efficiently, effectively, and pleasantly – exactly the kind of meeting that is most successful and that we all prefer.

How can you maintain a presence and a tone of voice that says that nothing disturbs you even when something unexpected pops up? It comes mainly from having prepared thoroughly. You will have worked out your overall plan for how meetings will eventually operate, even if you may not be inaugurating everything at once. You will also have prepared for each meeting in advance (as described especially in Chapters 3 through 5). Having prepared in this way will give you the confidence that allows you to be and to appear to be relaxed and comfortable, even while you are dealing with any difficult situation that might arise.

Some of the participants may carry over from previous board experience a tendency to expect and therefore to create tension in meetings. Even so, your personal example will whittle away at this tendency, meeting-after-meeting, until the new normal atmosphere for this board or committee is one of quiet collaboration in which differences of opinion can be expressed without negative emotions getting in the way.

You may ask how you go about enlisting this support. It is a fundamental truth that no one does well when taken by surprise, especially if he or she doesn't know the reasons for the surprise. So you do what you can to reduce the extent to which participants are surprised. And in addition to providing some warning about what is going to happen, you explain the reasons for it.

How you do this and over what period, depends upon your estimation of the organizational culture that you face. Chapter 1 pointed out that every organization has its own culture. Whatever the culture of the organization, you will be working within it.

From what you have read to this point it may have sounded as if the meeting will be what you single-handedly make of it. What you do will be important, but it will be only a part. The success of everything you plan and do will depend upon the extent to which you earn the support and active involvement of the other participants.

Asking: "Why the chair?"

Why do all of these responsibilities and tasks fall to you? The answer is that for at least three reasons you are the one person best suited to take them on.

First, you are probably the only one who has given much thought to how meetings can be redesigned. You are actively seeking ways to make them better; you are reading this book to find how this can be done. This contrasts with what is probably the attitude of most of the participants who often grumble about meetings but have given up hope of improving them.

Most board members will have relatively limited concepts of meetings, based on what they have observed in meetings that they have attended (or declined to attend). Considering the quality of many meetings, you can safely assume that much of what they have learned by observation includes some very unproductive assumptions and habits - assumptions and habits from which they often have to be weaned and from which you can free them.

The second reason that you are the person to lead the transformation is that you occupy the position in which you can actually put into practice the steps that you believe are desirable and possible.

The third reason is that the fact that you were selected for this position shows that people trust you – trust that is essential in leading any transformation.

Much of what the successful chair does is so unobtrusive that it goes almost unnoticed by the participants. But what the participants will notice after the transformations that you will introduce, is that the meetings have become brisk, pleasant, and productive. In time the participants become aware that through some unidentifiable alchemy, these enjoyable, successful meetings exist because of what the chair has done and is doing.

In all three basic roles, you are a leader. The essence of leadership is to stay ahead of those who follow but not so far ahead (or behind) as to lose them.

A LEADER IN NAME ONLY

There is a story that is supposedly set during the French Revolution.

A frantic, disheveled man rushes up to some people standing on a street corner.

"Which way did the mob go? I have to find them. I'm their *leader.*"

It is no wonder that the story refers to a mob, because that is what a group can become if it has a "leader" who has lost touch with those who are supposedly being led.

In facilitating, managing, and mentoring, you are truly a leader. But in the context of meetings, with leading come some special concepts and requirements.

Participating in discussion

The extent to which as chair you can actively participate in discussion depends largely on the size of the meeting. If there are more than perhaps a dozen participants, the answer is clear. When you are presiding at such a meeting, you absolutely do not express your opinions, suggest solutions, or answer questions (except those relating to meeting procedures).

There are good reasons for this strict prohibition.

Chairing a sizable meeting is a demanding task. It takes your full concentration to keep the discussion focused on the topics being considered; to be aware of and to handle amendments and procedural motions; to keep track of who is entitled to speak next; and above all, to sense the prevailing mood of the participants and decide what, if anything, you should be doing about it.

Regardless of how skilled you may be in the art of chairing, you cannot adequately concentrate on these demanding tasks if your mind is busy planning what you are going to say next and how it relates to what has been said by others. A large meeting in which the chair is distracted in this way is sure to become unfocussed and muddled, needlessly time-consuming, and frustrating for its participants.

So the wise chair of a relatively large meeting *does not take part in discussion*, in order to perform the tasks that only the chair can do – those that involve presiding at the meeting.

In smaller meetings, having perhaps a dozen or fewer participants, the tasks of presiding still take much of your attention, but they are less demanding than in a larger meeting. There are fewer participants to keep track of and because there are fewer participants, the range of opinions may be more limited. In addition, small meetings are and can safely be less formal and more relaxed than in larger meetings so it is easier to manage procedural matters.

Consequently, when chairing a *small* board or committee, when there is reason to do so the chair may join in discussion *in a limited way*.

Why would your participation need to be limited even if the group is relatively small? Probably the reason you have been chosen as the chair is that you are seen as having a particularly strong interest and special knowledge about the matters that will constitute the group's work. This perception will give your opinions more weight than those of other participants.

You do not want your personal opinions to carry so much weight that they effectively discourage other participants from expressing their views.

So, as chair of a small group in which you feel you can take some part in discussion, before expressing your opinion on a subject you wait until most of the other participants have already done so. Then you decide whether you *need* to add something important that has been overlooked. If everything relevant has already been said, repeating the same points won't contribute much to the discussion. It is only when you believe that you can contribute something different and important that it makes any sense for you to join the discussion.

So, when chairing even a small meeting, you limit the extent to which you allow yourself to take part in discussion.

Your restraint in this regard has another significant benefit – it protects you from seeming to be supporting too strongly any one position over another.

Maintaining impartiality

One measure of successful chairing is to be seen as having treated everyone fairly. It is not enough just to act fairly. For success as a chair, the other participants must have the sense that you *are* treating everyone fairly. How can you make sure of this? Some writers have said that the chair must be *objective* about issues being discussed.

To be objective means to be detached and not interested in the outcome. One reason that you accepted the position as chair is that you are interested in and care about the organization and what happens in it. So both because you care and because you have opinions about matters that affect the organization, you cannot, by definition, be objective.

If you can't be objective, how can you still be fair in your actions? The answer is that you can be *impartial*. You can take care not to let your wishes and opinions unfairly influence what you say and what you do as chair. And this self-discipline is needed not just during the meeting but also in the lead-up to it and in its follow-up.

It is not easy to remain impartial. You can only accomplish it if you continually keep in mind that you are not and cannot be objective. Remembering this sobering truth will help you to be doubly careful and sometimes even act against your personal inclinations. This will be especially when discussion becomes somewhat heated or when your own feelings are especially aroused as they inevitably will be at times.

What does acting impartially mean in practice? A simple example is that in chairing the meeting, you give equal opportunity to each participant regardless of whether you agree or disagree with what is likely to be said.

In addition, during the discussion you are careful not to betray by your facial expression or body language either agreement or disagreement with what others are saying. If you do decide to take a position, you hold off on doing so until most other participants have had their say.

Your caution in joining the discussion also protects you from being misunderstood. No matter how even-handedly you act, if you have revealed a preference for one position over another, the participants may unthinkingly assume that you are driving the meeting to some decision you have already made.

From this, without realizing it, they may assume that you are unfairly treating participants who hold positions that differ from yours. People have a strong natural preference for fairness. They resent it when they think someone is being treated unfairly, even if they don't agree with the person they see as the victim.

So, preserving your impartiality is another reason for limiting the extent to which you participate in discussion when chairing even a small meeting.

Getting around the "expert" shadow

The added respect accorded to your comments because you are chair will be even more pronounced if you are seen in any way as the expert or the boss.

In a volunteer organization in which the position of chair changes on a regular basis, this additional weighting may be largely overcome, as suggested above, by simply holding back on entering the discussion of a topic until most other participants have had their say.

In a business or professional or political meeting, however, the hierarchy shapes all relationships. If you happen to be a professional in the organization's area of primary interest – such as a psychologist in a social services group or a rabbi or minister or other member of the clergy in a religious organization – the effect is even more pronounced. Therefore, more attention has to be paid to this hazard. You want to leave the way open for other participants to feel comfortable taking any position that might be seen as disagreeing with that of the expert or the boss. Yet, freedom to differ is the very reason the meeting is being held – to get the unvarnished opinions of all those present.

In this circumstance, even when you postpone expressing an opinion, as soon as you finally reveal your position those who have spoken earlier may be tempted to tweak the position they originally expressed so that it conforms to yours.

How can you prevent this? There is no perfect answer, but if you find that other participants are catering too much to your opinions – and especially if they hold back on expressing an opinion until they hear yours – you have no choice. You will need to take prompt, corrective action.

As in many difficult situations the best remedy may be indirect. After having waited for others to speak about a topic, occasionally when it is appropriate, you could say something like, "When I first thought about this topic, I thought ... but now that I've heard the discussion, I see that I was wrong."

Such an admission goes a long way to humanizing the chair and allowing others to treat your comments just like those of other participants. It also helps to establish an atmosphere in which participants can accept it comfortably and not become defensive when others disagree with them.

If the problem seems too ingrained to be solved indirectly, you might give thought to a unique solution that was found by one highly successful facilitator-manager-mentor.

BORROWING AN IDEA FROM MEDIEVAL KINGS

I was discussing with James, a close friend, the problem of participants being too influenced by anything that he said, just because he was the boss as well as the expert.

For many years he had been a senior civil servant and was well experienced in chairing meetings large and small. His work required him to hold frequent meetings with a sizable number of directors, division heads, and project managers, all of whom were directly or indirectly accountable to him.

In these meetings James had become extremely frustrated because he wanted fresh ideas from those with whom he was meeting, but they all hung back until they could guess what direction he was leaning. Then some of them would rush forward to support whatever position they guessed that he held.

He tried everything, but he just couldn't seem to encourage the participants to take the risk of making suggestions that might disagree with his views.

Finally, he drew on his reading as a history buff and took an idea from the medieval kings. Before one meeting, he appointed one of the senior managers as "Court Jester." That individual's task, somewhat like that of the court jesters in a medieval king's court, was to make fun of whatever the king had said. But within the jokes there was often a critique that no one otherwise would have dared to mention.

At first people were shocked, but soon they got the idea. Eventually it led to a lot of hilarity. The experiment worked even better than James had hoped. So he appointed a new court jester at every meeting, and soon people were vying for the task. The important result, however, was that it made everyone comfortable with the possibility of disagreeing with the expert/boss. As a result, it encouraged fresh thinking and new ideas - exactly what James had wanted.

Not surprisingly, at a holiday party a year later the staff voted James the best boss they had ever had. And it must have been in part because they had learned through his rather bizarre innovation that their opinions were sought after and respected.

Explaining the advantages

How can you show that what you propose will be better for the participants? Easy. In many cases the most obvious result and the one that will be most appreciated will be that meetings will be shorter, while accomplishing more.

When you explain this in advance to the participants some will be skeptical, believing that this might be possible for other people's meetings, but that for some unexamined reason *their* meetings cannot be completed without running on and on. Still, when they see it actually happen they will be more ready to accept your other innovations.

Another benefit will be that discussions will be more focused and decisions will be clearer. And when a decision is made it will be recorded in such a way that it can be referred to easily in the future and have the desired continuing impact on the organization as a whole. These benefits will not be seen immediately, but they will become evident over time.

Even in an organization with a relatively inflexible culture you may be lucky enough to find that several of the board members are not firmly entrenched in it. In that case you may be able to go ahead and introduce a number of the innovations you have in mind right away, explaining each one briefly as you go along.

More likely, most of the board members will be representative of the organizational culture, and if it is even somewhat inflexible they too will require more complete warning and explanation before you introduce anything new.

Earning the support of the participants

Probably some members of the current board will have served on the board that preceded the present one. You will be showing them that your proposals will make for better meetings than before. Then it is logical for them to think: *The chair is saying that some new ways will be better than before. This must mean that there was something wrong with what we were doing before.*

No one likes to feel criticized or to be told they were wrong. So it would not take much for this thought to lead to resentment and opposition.

Even if all the participants are new to this group, probably many of the new members will have served on other boards, or at least they will have observed them in action (or perhaps, inaction). As a result, they will have picked up assumptions about "how things are done." They may need almost as much relearning as if they were carryover members and were clinging to past practices of this group in its previous form.

To forestall this sort of backlash, you will want to give careful thought to how to present your ideas and introduce new methods.

Acknowledging possible special sensitivities

The possible sensitivity felt by carryover board members will be especially likely to arise if, as in some organizations, the bylaws provide for the past chair to be a member of the subsequent - now the current - board.

If you face this situation, you may find it softens one possible source of resistance if you meet privately with the past chair before you explain to the other participants what you have in mind. To avoid premature disclosure, it will be safest to have this personal get-together no more than a day or so before you expose your plans to the rest of the participants.

You explain to the past chair that you are uncertain exactly how to proceed and want to ask for help in working out how best to introduce your plan to *try* some new methods.

The ideal outcome would be for the former chair to agree to work with you to explain your plans to the other participants. Next best would be for the past chair to give you some good advice, such as who might be most amenable and who the most resistant to what you will be proposing. But even if the former chair doesn't actively assist you, the fact that you sought advice may offset any indication of criticism and soften possible resentment.

And, of course, regardless of whether the past chair is present or absent, you are careful to concentrate your thoughts and your comments on what is good about the new methods, without commenting unfavorably on past practices. As the new methods demonstrate their worth, the contrast will be apparent without you having to spell out the comparison.

Introducing new methods through an orientation workshop

Although a quick once-over to explain your plans may be sufficient for an unusually adaptable board, in most cases you will sense that it will be better to proceed more deliberately.

Probably the best way to introduce the new methods is to conduct a full-fledged, half-day orientation workshop. So that all board members will receive the same information at the same time, it is important to schedule the date and time so that all of the participants can attend.

It is appropriate to refer to this event as a workshop. For it to be fully successful, it will be important for each member to take an active part. It cannot be an occasion in which one person – in this case you, the chair – delivers a lecture that explains everything, while the members absorb it passively. You will lead, but you will not lecture; the other participants will actively work.

"When I agreed to be on this board, I didn't realize we would have to make decisions."

In order for you to assume leadership to the extent necessary in the circumstances, you will be stepping out of your normal role as chair. You will still be facilitating, but your main influence will be as mentor, leading the other participants actively and directly.

How can you do this and still maintain the chair's neutrality? The simple answer is: You can't. Unlike discussion in a normal meeting, where you carefully *avoid* pushing the group to a conclusion that you have decided upon, in this case you know exactly where you want and expect the discussion to end up. In this special case you are not and cannot be neutral.

So you ask another member of the board who might be comfortable chairing, to preside during *this workshop*. This frees you to take a full part in presenting your proposals and in discussing them. And it demonstrates clearly the contrast between your actions when you are presenting a plan and when later, in a normal meeting, you are presiding.

To highlight the difference between your approach to a workshop and your actions as chair of a regular meeting, it may be helpful to hold the orientation workshop in a location that is different and more social than your normal meeting place. Unlike a normal meeting you might wish to start with beverages and snacks to create an informal atmosphere.

Designing the orientation workshop

You will probably find that the topics to be covered divide themselves naturally into three distinct but interrelated segments.

The first segment deals with how the board relates to the parent organization. The organization may have a Mission Statement, which can serve as a starting point. Unfortunately, however, most such statements consist of general expressions of good intentions rather than of specific commitments to action. The orientation may be more informative if you focus primarily on the question of how *the participants* would describe the organization's purposes. Equally revealing is to query how the participants believe the organization is perceived in the wider community.

This discussion should naturally lead to the question of how the board relates internally to the organization's existing committees, task forces, and project activities. Exploring this question effectively defines one of the primary responsibilities of the board. In fact, many of the other board functions flow from its relationship to its parent organization.

This first segment may need something like one-half to three-quarters of an hour. The participants will not yet be tired, but it may still be wise to call a ten-minute break for which you suggest that everyone stand up, walk around a bit, refill their coffee/tea/juice, and then return to their seats, refreshed and ready to go on.

The second workshop segment will depend more than the first upon information you will need to provide. It covers the structure and functions of the board meetings. It will start with a description of how the agenda will be put together and how major topics will be chosen *for discussion and decision* (see Chapter 3). This emphasis explains the need to allocate timing so the meeting doesn't have to run too long.

There also needs to be an explanation of the prompt disposal of those items that do not require lengthy discussion (for which see Chapters 3 and 4). To avoid later surprises it will probably be helpful to explain how reports will be handled and why this will be so (for which also see Chapter 3).

This will probably be a good time to initiate discussion of how a motion, while not always required, can often help to bring discussion to a sharp focus. This emphasis offers an easy transition to a brief explanation of why the minutes will now report actions and decisions rather than attempting to capture what has been said in discussion (as explained in detail in Chapter 9).

After another brief break, you will tackle the third segment. It could be described as "How we deal with each other." This discussion will probably be most effective if you ask the participants to break up into sub-groups of three or four members each. These sub-groups will each work independently to come up with the elements that make for good interpersonal relationships. They will each consider such matters as taking turns speaking, not interrupting others, avoiding harshly personal critical terms, and pleasantly keeping the focus on the business at hand.

With some guidance from you some sub-groups might include a commitment not to engage in talk outside of the meeting about what has happened within it – that is "triangulation" – as described elsewhere in this chapter.

Each sub-group is likely to take a somewhat different tack, so when the whole group reassembles to report their results, the combination will probably provide the ingredients for an excellent Code of Conduct (as also described in this chapter).

You finish by explaining your role as chair, with special emphasis on how you will limit your participation in discussion, in order to focus on conducting the meeting. This will probably come as a new concept to many of the participants since they will usually have seen people who preside at meetings taking the dominant part in presenting proposals and in discussing them.

When the participants have this new understanding of the role of the chair, later they will be less likely during a meeting to wait for you to carry the discussion. And it makes the point that overall responsibility for the meeting rests with them as well as with you.

Usually such a workshop ends with a social time or even a potluck meal so everyone can relax, enjoy each other's company, and take pride in having framed the future meetings for success.

In the future when new members join the board, they come in at a disadvantage. The continuing members will already have had the explanations in the orientation session. Further, over several months they have become used to the new culture of the board. Anyone coming in new faces this new-to-them culture that may surprise and confuse them and be quite overwhelming and even intimidating.

So, whether you have another similar orientation session for several new members at once or one-on-one informal conversation with a single new member, it will be important to cover much the same material with them.

De-mystifying parliamentary rules

Even if you are completely successful in enlisting support from all of the participants for your planned modifications, in some circumstances you may find a meeting entangled in procedural misunderstandings. You can take steps to keep this from happening.

Even the most experienced and sophisticated of chairs may sometimes feel overwhelmed by the mere thought of parliamentary rules of order. After all, if the authors of *Robert's Rules of Order Newly Revised* need 716 pages to explain the rules,[1] what chance has the average chair of mastering them?

In fact, that is the wrong question. The real question is: What does the chair *need* to know to manage a meeting? A meeting of a board or other small group is, and should be, relatively informal. Knowledge of a few basic principles, coupled with common sense and good will, meet the requirement. Those principles are set out in a page and a half in Appendix B and can be easily absorbed in a few minutes.

A slightly more complete understanding will be required to manage an Annual General Meeting or an even larger convention, but this too will not require long study. The same appendix includes a summary of the procedural steps that will probably be the only ones you will ever encounter in even the most formal meetings that you will need to chair. This appendix also provides a quick guide to whether each of these steps may be open for discussion and which ones require more than a majority for adoption.

If you foresee that a large meeting will become contentious, however, you may find it advisable to have the organization retain a practicing parliamentarian to advise you during the meeting.

(This is not to discourage you from studying to become a qualified professional parliamentarian yourself. Instead, it is to point out that short of this, there are ways you can quickly and easily acquire enough knowledge to function as chair without being tripped up or embarrassed.)

This leads to the question of exactly what modifications, innovations, and new concepts you will be introducing. The best place to start is with the agenda, so that is the subject of the next chapter.

1 Robert's Rules of Order, Newly Revised, 11 ed. (12th edition scheduled to be released in September 2023.)

Chapter 3

Designing an Agenda That Works For You

No matter what the organizational culture is and regardless of the pace at which you decide to introduce new methods, the first and most far-reaching impact will be from the modifications you will be making to the agenda.

Recognizing the agenda's importance

Many people think of an agenda as nothing more than a simple listing of topics that will be brought up at the meeting. In fact, if thoughtfully designed, it can be much more than that. Most participants will not have given an agenda much thought, so you can usually modify it as much as you wish without raising resistance.

A well-designed agenda can help to keep the meeting on track, set its tone, keep it flexible but orderly, and shape it so that it accomplishes what is expected of it. The agenda's layout will facilitate the prompt disposal of routine, non-controversial matters, saving precious time for discussion of the major topics. It will be structured so the meeting will be completed within a reasonable time, while still allowing for full, comfortable participation.

You may ask how a simple page could have all of these wonderful effects and in addition help the meeting to complete its work within its planned time frame.

The answer is that through the agenda the meeting's emphasis will be kept on the important topics, and not scattered among other matters. As you will discover, this emphasis will make the agenda a wise chair's best friend.

In this chapter we'll look at what goes into an agenda. The following chapters will then cover some of the procedures that keep the meeting moving, to make the best use of the participants' time.

Since the purpose of the meeting is to discuss and make decisions about major topics, we should start with how they can best be handled.

Selecting the major topics to include

The first task in building the agenda is to decide which major topics should be discussed and decided upon during the meeting.

In any active organization there will always be a large number of topics that could be placed before the board or committee for discussion and decision. If all were to be included, however, they would flood the meeting, allowing little time for each one to be fully explored.

Many of these topics can be handled by other groups or even by specific individuals. If they can reasonably be diverted elsewhere, board meetings can be reserved for the most important topics – those that have the greatest impact on the organization as a whole.

How can you evaluate which topics to include and which to divert elsewhere or delete entirely? A friend of mine offers a method to make this crucial selection.

APPLYING TWO TESTS

Leigh, a close friend, is an internationally acclaimed consultant who helps transnational corporations to restructure themselves for greater effectiveness. I asked her how she could make best use of her time by screening out the topics that are of least importance in order to focus on those that make the biggest difference.

"Simple," she said. "I ask two questions: Who cares? and So what?"

At first I thought she was joking. Then I realized the power in these two questions. If no one will be seriously affected by a topic, no one will care about it, and it should not take up anyone's time. As for the second question, if the topic doesn't have much impact, it does not deserve attention, either.

So, after my first surprise at the apparent simplicity of Leigh's test questions, I came to realize that they could work to select topics for a meeting agenda.

Many boards are content to leave these choices to whoever is chairing the meeting, perhaps working in conjunction with the secretary.

But if the meeting is to be owned by the participants – an objective that we have already discussed – they should be given the opportunity to help select what topics will be included in the agenda and therefore in the meeting. So, ten days or so before a regular monthly meeting, you make a short list of perhaps up to half a dozen major topics that need to be addressed.

You send this list to the participants, asking if they have any other major topics that they believe need to be *discussed and decisions made* about them. This is a reminder to the members that the meeting is for these two purposes and is not a platform for general conversation. There are places for casual chitchat, but a board meeting is not one of them.

Also, although it is stated in casual terms, your invitation refers to "the next couple of days" as a loose deadline within which you are asking the participants to respond. This reflects the unwritten but important principle that whenever an action is requested or planned, it should be framed so that it includes reference to when it is expected to be accomplished, whether that time be anything from one hour to several years.

You will probably know which topics are currently most important for the organization, so you will have included them in your list. If your list is inclusive, the participants are not likely to suggest additions. If, though, they make any suggestions, having learned of them now gives you time to include them in the agenda, or to explain why you don't think they should be added. Whether there are any suggestions or not, your inquiry has had the benefit of reminding the participants that it is *their* meeting and that they are responsible for it.

Occasionally, in response to your invitation, a member may suggest a topic that for some reason would be inappropriate for the meeting. Perhaps this subject matter is the responsibility of another group or individual; perhaps it has already been decided and there has been no change that would require the decision to be revisited; perhaps it is something that should be delegated to another individual or group decision-maker, saving time for the board.

Having uncovered it this early, you have time to go to the participant who has suggested it and explain why it shouldn't be included. If the person is not convinced, you can include the topic in the agenda, leaving it to the group to decide during the meeting whether they think it is something that they should be discussing.

Then comes an important question: How should each topic be worded on the agenda to ensure the broadest, most open discussion of it?

Wording the major topics to avoid limiting discussion

Communications experts have studied how people's understanding and discussion of a topic will depend on how it is "framed." One important aspect of this framing is the choice of wording used to describe the topic. The words we choose may freeze the discussion along certain lines, without anyone recognizing that this is what has happened.

As an impartial chair you want to encourage the other board members to think broadly about a question and not to jump to the first solution that comes to mind. To help with this desired openness, you want to keep from unintentionally describing a major topic in such a way that it narrows the scope of the discussion about it.

To avoid this narrowing of scope, you can use a tool that is called the "Focus Sentence" to guide you in wording the topic on the agenda.

To try it out, you select one of the major topics that will be discussed in the meeting. To illustrate, let's suppose that your organization has been experiencing a marked decline in its overall membership, and that you believe this situation should be discussed at the next board meeting and some decisions made about it.

Using this tool, you start by writing a sentence that begins with the words: "This meeting will...." and go on to identify the topic to be discussed.

As a first draft for our example you might write something like:

This meeting will plan a campaign to attract new members.

This wording, or framing, would get the discussion off to a discussion about how to plan and carry out a membership campaign and its possible advantages and disadvantages.

When you take a second look at this Focus Sentence, it will probably come to you that a membership campaign is not the only way to approach the declining membership. Yet, if the agenda topic is worded in this way, you, as chair, have decided that there *will be* a membership campaign. Then all that is left for the board to do is to rubber stamp your conclusion and to design the campaign.

You see that this wording closes out other innovative ideas that otherwise the board members might bring to the question. So, it's back to the drawing board, to write a revised draft of the Focus Sentence.

After a few moments thought, your revised Focus Sentence might read something like:

This meeting will consider how to reverse the declining membership.

That's more open to new ideas and less directive. But is it open enough?

Suppose that as you think about it you recall that some members have said that they think the organization was actually stronger when it had fewer members, but more of them were fully engaged in the organization's activities. You don't necessarily agree with them, but in keeping with your commitment to the chair's impartiality, you don't want to foreclose their point of view.

So, you look again at the Focus Sentence. Now your third draft might read:

This meeting will consider responses to the declining membership.

This wording - the new framing - encourages the broader consideration that would not have been as likely had you not moved away from the first wording with its focus on a membership campaign. Now, instead of the agenda item reading, "Membership campaign," or the second draft's "*Problems* of declining membership," it will read "Declining membership." With this more open wording you are putting the situation to the participants without having decided for them whether this is a problem or not, and you certainly haven't restricted their thinking to a membership campaign.

As chair, you certainly have given a lot of thought to the problems of your organization and naturally have thought of possible solutions. It takes self-awareness and care to keep from reflecting your own solutions as you guide the meeting. Using a Focus Sentence for how you will describe each of the major topics, you can word the lines on the agenda to keep the discussion open and free ranging.

(And don't worry that the wider discussion will take too much meeting time; Chapter 4 will cover that concern.)

Choosing the order of the major topics

Now you have selected which topics to include, and how to word each one. You could just list them in any order on the agenda. But the order you place them in can have an effect on the mood of the meeting, and on how it progresses.

It sets a good mood for the meeting if you choose as the first major topic one that is relatively noncontroversial and that can be resolved rather quickly and with little fuss. An easy agreement gives unspoken but clear messages to the participants:

- As a group we keep our attention on the topic being discussed;
- We work together to solve problems;
- The questions we discuss *can be answered;* and
- We solve problems quickly, pleasantly, and effectively.

When a meeting starts positively, the good mood tends to persist throughout the meeting. By way of contrast, if the first major topic is quite controversial and takes a long time to resolve, it may leave at least mild discomfort among the participants. Once a negative mood develops it tends to persist throughout the meeting just as does a positive mood.

So you list an easy topic first, immediately after the routine opening items.

The second major topic should be the one that you expect to be the most difficult or controversial, especially if it might raise strong emotions. Since the meeting mood has already been set by the easy first topic, any rough spots that arise during discussion of the second will have less impact on the subsequent meeting mood than it would have if it had been first.

Addressing a tough topic relatively early in the meeting also has the advantage that the participants attack it while they are fresh, which usually translates into "more flexible, and more forgiving" – desirable traits for a meeting and especially for one dealing with a difficult topic.

After you have chosen the two major topics for places one and two, the remaining major topics can be in almost any order, although to the extent convenient it may be helpful to try to alternate difficult and easy topics. Also, sometimes discussion of a topic has to wait for a decision on another topic, so the dependence of the one on the other dictates the respective orders of the two.

It may be best to leave another easy topic for last so the participants can go home after the meeting basking in the good feeling that comes from collaboration and agreement.

Now you have decided which topics to include, how to word them, and the order in which to place them. During the meeting, how will you open discussion?

Inviting someone to present a topic?

For some topics all you will need to do is to refer to "the next item on the agenda" and to read aloud the agenda line.

An occasional topic, however, may have required someone to have assembled for the participants some explanatory or background information. In this case, you may feel it would be courteous to invite the person who has done this work to present the topic to the meeting.

Unfortunately, such a thoughtful gesture may backfire. In a sense this is like asking the person to sponsor the topic. In such a situation, some people become so enthusiastic about the topic that they ramble on about it for longer than is necessary. The apparent sponsor may also go further and present "the obvious solution" to it, effectively narrowing the possibilities for open discussion. You have struggled with a Focus Sentence to keep discussion free-ranging, so you don't want to have this work undone by someone presenting a one-sided or predetermined view.

A more effective and safer approach will be, before the meeting, to ask the person who assembled the information to write the relevant background facts in point form. It can be put in the hands of the participants before the meeting, (as will be discussed in Chapter 5). Then you can ask the person who assembled the information to be prepared during the meeting to answer questions that the participants may ask for clarification.

And, of course, you can acknowledge and express the *group's* (not the *chair's*) appreciation for the work done in gathering the material.

Handling emergency topics

At some time in your service as chair you may be faced with the need for emergency action. This might occur when a question arises that is so important and so urgent that the board has to deal with it immediately. In such an extremely rare situation, the urgency may be such that there could be serious consequences if the decision were to await the next scheduled meeting of the board.

You see that you have to call a special meeting of the board. You let all board members know the nature of the emergency, and that it will be the only topic on the agenda for this special meeting. Then you work with each member to find the best date and time for a meeting so that *all* can attend.

If it is not possible to find such a date and time within the period in which the decision has to be made, the special meeting will have to be arranged when the most members possible can participate. Not only must a large enough number be present to qualify as a quorum, but the timing should be set to accommodate as many additional members as possible.

For the meeting to be valid you will also have to prepare a form that *all* members will sign, which gives consent for the meeting to be held with less-than-required advance notice.

This may seem like considerable extra effort, and it is. But such a true emergency arises so seldom that it will not often place the additional burden on you and the other participants.

Allowing for last-minute topics

Now that we have covered the rare true emergency, we must also make plans to handle another kind of situation that some people may hope to have treated as if it were a genuine emergency. This is the situation in which one or more participants, or even non-members, come up with a topic that they didn't think of early enough to have it placed on the agenda but that they now hope will be tended to immediately. This can become an emotional issue, but there is a way to manage it comfortably.

In such a case, unless you are prepared for this to happen occasionally, as chair your first thought might be that you have only two possible options – to accept the new topic or to refuse to do so.

If you allow it to be shoehorned into the pre-planned agenda, you would be letting it disrupt careful planning that you and others have done for the meeting. The new topic would take meeting time away from the other business that needs to be covered.

Inserting a new, unplanned topic at this time may also require the participants to make a decision on it for which no one was prepared and for which relevant information may not have been made available.

Clearly, it is not a good option to allow such an unexpected topic to disrupt the agenda and the meeting.

The other apparent option is to refuse to accept the new topic. Your refusal may antagonize the person(s) demanding to be heard. It might also set you up to be seen as a dictator who decides what will and will not be part of "your" meeting. So this is another bad option.

You don't have to accept either bad option. The solution is to recognize in advance that this sort of interruption may occasionally arise and to make plans to handle it. You provide an outlet by placing a line in every agenda labeled, "Items Received Too Late for the Agenda."

On the rare occasion when someone is insistent on bringing up a topic that doesn't appear on the agenda, you smile sweetly and say, "This new topic will be taken up as the subject matter of the agenda line for 'Items Received Too Late for the Agenda.'"

You have handled the unexpected intrusion, allowing the meeting to follow the agenda as if there had been no interruption and at the same time you have accommodated those who have demanded the opportunity to bring up the late topic. It's a win all around.

The title of this line item also reminds the interrupters that they *did* propose the topic *too late*. The agenda line is placed so it will come up near the end of the meeting, so discussion of it is necessarily limited. The situation is a not-very-subtle but unobjectionable suggestion that if someone wishes a topic to be thoroughly discussed, it would be wise to advise the chair early enough for it to be included in the agenda.

Not surprisingly, this method has shown that its use greatly reduces the frequency of such mid-meeting interruptions.

Because participants have had the opportunity well before the meeting to suggest new topics, they will seldom need to suggest additions at the last minute. So usually this agenda line will not be needed for its named purpose. This leaves it for a valuable cushion of flexibility in the timing for other items. It easily allows them to run slightly over their allotted times without causing the meeting to be extended beyond its scheduled closure. (For the explanation of methods to control timing, see Chapter 4.)

Making use of the headings

Now we will be considering how the agenda looks.

It will make the rest of this chapter more clear if we follow a model agenda. The one that follows on the next page might be for the board meeting of a hypothetical not-for-profit organization. We'll start at the top and work our way downward.

At the top of the agenda are the headings – the name of the organization; type of meeting; location, date and time; and the fact that this is an agenda.

If the time and place of the meeting vary from meeting to meeting, stating them in the agenda heading can help to prevent misunderstanding. If these items don't change from month to month, however, the information still serves as a useful reminder. Busy people may have several meetings in a month and can easily confuse the meeting time or even location of one group with that of another.

Although it may seem like a duplication to include both the date and the day of the week, there is good reason to do so. People tend to remember the day of the week better than they do a simple date. And how many times have you received a notice about something in which the date is accidentally misstated, for example, 12 instead of 11? Including both helps to catch any misstatement. It doesn't take space away from anything else, so why not include both?

Including these identifying details also serves as a reminder to the participants when they receive the agenda several days before the meeting. Stating the time of the meeting reminds them that the meeting is scheduled for that time and that it will actually start exactly at that time.

In Chapter 4 we'll cover the suggested times that appear in the left-hand column. But the first matters that need our attention are some items that must be provided for in a well-planned meeting.

The following is an example of the agenda for a hypothetical community organization.

FRIENDS OF THE MUSEUM (FOM)
BOARD OF DIRECTORS
Regular Meeting, 7:00 p.m. Thursday, November 21, 2xxx
Westwood Community Hall

AGENDA

Suggested <u>Times</u>		
7:00	Call to Order Acknowledgement of Quorum (Reporting the names of unavoidable absentees?) *Approval of the agenda (Recognition of Visitors?) *Approval of Minutes, Regular Meeting of October 17, 2xxx	CHAIR
7:02	*Consent Register	CHAIR
7:03	*Education Committee, Recommendation #1, Reception for Dignitaries	
7:09	*Recommendation #2, Public Forum on Projects	
7:27	*If Forum approved*, task force to select panelists	
7:31	*If Forum approved*, facilities, publicity, arrangements	
7:39	*FoM declining membership; possible causes	
7:47	Implications for volunteers, budget, public awareness	
7:54	Possible actions re membership	
8:14	Honorary memberships and awards (confidential)	TONI
8:20	Items received too late for agenda	
8:28	Next meeting (Thursday, December 17?)	
8:29	Adjournment	CHAIR

** Relevant information was distributed in advance.*

Providing for the routine procedural topics

After the heading, the agenda proper starts with several items that need to be listed to remind you, as chair, to bring them up and to have them reflected in the minutes.

These routine items are:

- ✓ Call to order;
- ✓ Acknowledgement of quorum;
- ✓ Approval of the agenda;
- ✓ Recognition and introduction of visitors, *if relevant*; and
- ✓ Approval of minutes of previous meeting(s).

Calling these items "routine" does not mean that they are unimportant. Not at all. Each of them, except recognition of visitors, is necessary, but they are routine because they have to appear in every agenda. Even so, because of how they are handled they can be and should be disposed of quickly. We will consider each in turn.

Call to order

You probably would not need a reminder to call the meeting to order. However, there has to be a starting point for the timing that is allocated, (details of which will appear in Chapter 4). And it does no harm once again to remind the participants of the starting time. So it is a minor point, but is worth including.

Acknowledgement of the quorum

The mention of the quorum is a different matter; it is crucial. You know that the meeting can't proceed without a quorum, that is, the stated number of voting members who must be present, as established by the organization's bylaws, or by the applicable legislation. (If the organization's bylaws and the governing legislation differ, the valid quorum is the larger of the two. If both are silent as to quorum, the default number is a majority of the voting membership.)

The minutes of the meeting will include the fact that the chair stated that a quorum was present. The entry in the minutes gives an answer to anyone who might later challenge decisions taken during the meeting, on the ground that there might not have been enough members present to hold a valid meeting.

(Chapter 6 explains what to do if you find that there aren't enough participants present to meet the quorum requirement.)

Approval of the agenda

The next routine item is the approval of the agenda. The participants will have seen a draft of it several days prior to the meeting (as explained in Chapter 5), but in order for it to be official it has to be approved by the participants who are present. When they do so they have acknowledged that it is the roadmap for the meeting, and that it will be followed unless it is formally amended later in the meeting.

Recognition of visitors

If visitors usually appear at these meetings, or if you know that some visitors may attend a particular meeting, you may wish to include a line in the agenda to remind yourself as chair briefly to acknowledge their presence.

If a line about visitors is included in the agenda, it appears as the line *after* the line for approval of the agenda. There is a reason for this location. Once the agenda has been approved, the direction for the meeting has been established. It is then clear that there is no place for visitors to introduce a new topic unless it has been pre-arranged, (in which case it would have been included in the agenda).

Other suggestions for handling visitors will be discussed in Chapter 6, which covers the conduct of the early part of the meeting.

Approval of Minutes.

Next comes the approval of the minutes of the previous meeting. When the participants give their approval, they are saying that the words in the minutes accurately record what took place during the previous meeting. With this approval, the minutes become the official record of the earlier meeting. (The content and handling of minutes are covered in Chapter 9.)

These routine procedural items are essential but they cannot be allowed to take up more meeting time than they require. Disposing of them properly but promptly saves meeting time for the primary business of the meeting, which we keep constantly in mind; that is discussion of and making decisions about the major topics.

Dealing with reports from officers, committees, and others

You will have noticed that the agenda does not include any mention of reports from officers, staff members, or committees. Yet on some agendas that you have seen, lines for reports appear immediately after the routine procedural items.

In practice, reports tend to be extensive written accounts, often supplemented by oral repetition of exactly the same facts as are in the written portions. They take up large blocks of time, leaving little for the intentional purpose of the meeting - discussion of and decisions about the major topics.

Even more important, the primary focus of a report is to report (!) what has happened in the *past*, in contrast with the purpose of the meeting, which is to discuss and to make decisions about what may take place in the *future*.

It seems clear that typical reports are out of step with the purposes of the meeting. But you say, "Our board needs to know what has happened throughout the organization. How else can we know this without reports?"

Copyright 2002 by Randy Glasbergen.
www.glasbergen.com

"What software would you recommend to give my presentation so much flash and sizzle that nobody notices that I have nothing to say?"

The answer is not to dispense with reports but to handle them differently. As chair you can send all reports to the participants a few days before the meeting. This gives them time to read them deliberately at their convenience and to think about them and be ready to comment during the meeting, if they wish, concerning what the reports say.

If a report contains a recommendation, whatever it proposes will appear in the agenda as a separate line item. In this way the focus is on the recommendation and not on the account of past activities.

So, unlike many traditional agendas, the model agenda that appears in this chapter does not contain any reference to reports of officers or committees. In one stroke we have saved the meeting from a major time-waster and at the same time created an opportunity for the participants to read, absorb, and react to the contents of all reports.

Making effective use of financial statements

Some boards regularly handle reports from most committees and officers in the ways just described, but they make a special exception for current financial statements. The rationale for this exception is that since the board is responsible for keeping the organization financially healthy, (which it certainly is) it must devote large amounts of meeting time to financial reports in order to understand them.

What often results from this assumption is that the treasurer or chair of the Finance Committee is expected to read to the other participants a string of numbers selected from the detailed financial statements. But most members are not trained in accounting, and they take for granted that they can't understand financial reports. When they are confronted with pages of figures their eyes glaze over and their minds escape to somewhere else. This is not their fault; it is because of the ways in which financial information is often presented.

It doesn't have to be this way. Financial information can be presented in a way that is easily understood, and doesn't take up meeting time.

Appendix C explains in detail how you can work with the treasurer to do this. For this chapter about agendas, it is enough to state three interrelated fundamental practices:

- ✓ First, the treasurer or chair of the Finance Committee provides a summary of the relevant highlights and how they compare with the approved budget;
- ✓ Second, this summary accompanies the full financial reports, as they are sent to the members several days before the meeting; and
- ✓ Third, financial questions appear on the agenda if and only if decisions need to be made about them.

From this brief summary, it can be seen that financial statements are treated a bit differently from most other reports. Yet, like the other reports, the proposed methods make the participants better able to understand their contents, while conserving large amounts of meeting time.

Responding to the people who have been giving reports

When you first deal in this way with reports, some of the people who have been accustomed to providing lengthy reports may feel that they have lost a place in the limelight.

To help resolve any hurt feelings you can meet with each one in advance. In these private sessions you explain that you believe it is important for the board members to be able to grasp what has been in reports and that in the rush of a meeting it hasn't been possible to pay adequate attention to them. By providing the reports to the participants early, they can properly consider the important information they contain.

If someone has been accustomed to giving only an oral report, the private advance explanation is even more important. You can explain that experts in the field of learning have shown that people will understand and remember several times as much from a written statement as from one that is given orally. You ask the person who has been giving oral reports to write the facts in simple point-form. Then the members will be better able to understand and especially to remember what the report has said.

Reorganizing the handling of reports in this way will save large amounts of time in the meeting that can be more productively used for discussion and decision-making.

We can also dispense with some other agenda lines that often appear in traditional agendas.

Dispensing with "Old Business/New Business/Business Arising" lines

The modern agenda does not include lines for "Old Business" or "New Business" (or for "Business Arising from the Minutes" if it has been appearing in past agendas). A caption for Old Business can be misleading at best. If it is truly old business, it has already been disposed of in a previous meeting and does not need rehashing. On the other hand, if it is business that has been deferred from a previous meeting it will appear in its own right as an agenda line.

As for New Business, isn't all business in the meeting *new*? Then it doesn't need a separate caption. Each item to be discussed and decided will have its own line in the agenda so there's no need to group it under a general category of what is new.

A line for "Business Arising from the Minutes" has appeared in some old-fashioned agendas. There is no business that comes from the previous minutes except possibly for responsibilities that have been assigned to various people or groups. If it is necessary to check on what action has been taken in regard to these earlier decisions the follow-up will appear as a line item in the agenda. Otherwise, referring to past minutes is an unspoken invitation for participants to second-guess whatever was decided in the previous meeting. It also invites discussion of why the decision was made in the last meeting and probably also a repetition of that discussion, all for no particular benefit.

So, in the modern agenda, there is no place for these three outdated lines.

Completing the agenda

What remains are the last three items. First: "Items Received Too Late for the Agenda," which has been described fully above.

The final two lines are for confirming (or setting) the date, time, and location of the next meeting. Even if these details are the same from month to month, this line serves as a reminder. It also reminds participants to check their future commitments, so the group can make adjustments if several members will be unable to attend at the scheduled time. If time or location have to be arranged, it is much easier to do so while the participants are all together than by even the most innovative software for the purpose.

The chair's statement that the meeting is adjourned is needed so that there is a clear boundary between what occurred during the meeting and anything else that occurred immediately afterwards. Having this line in the agenda is again a helpful reminder for the chair not to overlook this important statement.

This completes the agenda, except for the timing, which will be covered in the next chapter, and for how and when you distribute it, which appears in Chapter 5.

Chapter 4

Making Best Use of Meeting Time

One of the most common complaints about meetings is that they run too long. This is often coupled with a comment such as, "We could have accomplished as much in half the time if we had kept our minds on what we were doing instead of spending so much time on other things."

In your combined roles as Facilitator, Manager, and Mentor, there is much that you can do to correct this often-legitimate complaint.

We can start with two techniques, which when practiced will save meaningful amounts of time during a typical meeting. Then this chapter will describe an overall approach that will help to allocate meeting time so that it is directed to where it does the most good and is not frittered away on nonessential tasks or diversions.

Approving by unanimous consent

First, we will describe a time-saving tool the knowledgeable chair can use frequently throughout the meeting.

This tool can be used in many cases when participants have reached agreement on a decision. When appropriate, it replaces the need for the chair to ask for a motion, then perhaps a second, then to invite discussion, then to take votes for and votes against, and finally to declare the motion approved. The time saved for a single topic is only a minute or so, but when it is used several times during a meeting, these minutes add up and save time for useful discussion of the main topics.

When is it appropriate to use approval by unanimous consent? The answer is when:

- ✓ all members have indicated their approval either by what they have said or by their comfortable silence; and
- ✓ the discussion of the issue has not been especially controversial.

When these two conditions are met, the chair's use of approval by unanimous consent will save time while reserving the democratic nature of the meeting.

"How can it be democratic," you may ask, "for a chair to announce that something has been approved, when the members haven't voted on it?"

An example is approval of the agenda. The draft agenda has been in the hands of the members for several days before the meeting (for details, see Chapter 5). They have had plenty of opportunity to question any aspect of it and to suggest additions or modifications. At the meeting you have offered them this opportunity once again.

So there's no need to go through what in the circumstances would be an artificial, time-consuming procedure that would not bring out any useful discussion or modifications.

Unanimous consent is also applicable for approval of any issue that has been discussed during the meeting, when the chair realizes that everyone – not just a majority – is in favor of the same solution to it. It is as democratic in such a circumstance for the chair to acknowledge this fact directly as it would be if the participants' hands were to be raised all around.

But there are limitations to its use. It should not be used when the topic has been controversial even though all participants have finally agreed on the same solution. After the meeting participants are likely to continue to think about or even talk about any decision that was made about a controversial topic. Those who originally supported it may later begin to have doubts about it. People's memories tend to be rather leaky; they may come to believe that they didn't *really* approve it during the meeting and that the chair was mistaken in thinking that the decision was unanimous.

So for important and sensitive topics, no matter how supportive the members may be during the meeting, it is safer to take an active vote rather using approval by consent.

In other matters, use of the procedure can be a valuable time-saver.

There is a secondary benefit that no one may notice, but that can improve participants' views of the chair and make it easier for the chair later to introduce other innovations. Whenever a chair is trying to bring some order out of general meeting chaos, often the participants who resist feel that the chair is hung up on parliamentary procedure. Using approval by consent to skip the formality of a motion and all that goes with it can show a welcome degree of flexibility to counteract this mistaken impression.

If there are members who question the legitimacy of declaring approval by unanimous consent, you can refer them to the current editions of the leading authorities on parliamentary procedure – *Robert's* (pages 54-56 and 474), The *Standard Code* (page 142), and *Cannon* (page 43). In every case, the authors recommend use of this method whenever it is appropriate.

This is a good start toward controlling meeting time. And it sets the pattern for the rest of the meeting. It says: "We will take the time necessary to do what needs to be done, but we won't waste time in unnecessarily formal methods when other legitimate ways are available."

From this point we can move on to more direct means of controlling meeting time. There is another, slightly more complicated, method that is appropriate in some situations.

Saving meeting time by using a Consent Register

Often an organization's bylaws or governing legislation require the board to approve specified types of decisions. These might include contracts for certain kinds of purchases or for greater-than-specified dollar amounts; employment of staff members for specified positions; purchase or sale of property; formal certification of requests for grants from or reports to various government agencies; or other specific situations.

Often for these required approvals the board relies unquestioningly on advice from other decision-making groups or from staff members. The board members don't really *decide*, they only *approve* formally to meet the technical requirement.

For such situations, by using a Consent Register the meeting can skip time-consuming procedure and pointless discussion when that discussion won't make any difference anyway. (The listing may also be called a Consent Agenda or a Consent Calendar.)

How does it work?

As chair you gather each of the items for which the board will be relying solely on advice from someone else who has reviewed it and is telling the board that it is correct and should be approved. As you list each item you refer to who it is that is recommending it. You also include a brief note as to why board approval is needed.

A week or so before the scheduled meeting, when you send your request to the board members for possible topics to add to the agenda, you include a draft of the Consent Register that you propose to put before the meeting.

You ask if any board member has a question or reservation about any of the items listed. If even one member has a question or comment on an item, you immediately remove it from the Consent Register and add it to the regular agenda. Then everyone understands that later, during the meeting, there will be no questions or discussion about any of the items that remain on the Consent Register.

FRIENDS OF THE MUSEUM (FOM)

CONSENT REGISTER

For Board Meeting March 13, 2xxx

ITEM	APPROVAL RECOMMENDED BY
Invoice, Carey Roofing, $3,427.86 (Final payment, roof repairs)	Susan McClary, Chair, Building Committee
Appointment, temporary bookkeeper, John Wilson, (Fill-in for bookkeeper's maternity leave)	Carlos Fernandez, Chair, Human Resources Committee
Application for tax abatement	Jeanne LaPierre, Treasurer

In accordance with FoM policy, this Consent Register will be approved by a single motion, seconded and approved. Then the minutes will record each item separately as having been approved unanimously by the board.

Early in the meeting, you take up the Consent Register from the agenda as a single item, without making any further reference to the individual items listed on it. When its turn comes up, you ask for a single motion to approve the whole list.

You take one vote for the Consent Register as a whole. Since everyone has already indicated that no discussion is needed for any of the items, they will unanimously approve the Consent Register, and thus, all of the individual items listed on it. And all in one motion and one vote.

Through this procedure you have saved the meeting valuable time that would have been taken if there had been even brief discussion of each item listed and each had needed approval of a motion, followed by what would have been an automatic vote without any meaningful discussion.

Following is a typical example of a Consent Register for the board of a hypothetical community organization.

As chair you can introduce these two techniques - approval by unanimous consent and the Consent Register - at almost any time. Each will make a difference in how meeting time will be spent. The greatest effect on meeting time, however, will come from specific allocations, minute by minute, which we will now begin to address.

Setting the maximum meeting length

As has been mentioned, the most common complaint about meetings is that they last too long. We all agree that time is valuable, and if lost can never be regained. Yet we often act as though we forget this truth when it comes to meetings.

All too often, a meeting is scheduled for two, two-and-a-half, or even three hours. In other cases, even if not planned this way, a meeting may drift on for this long before it finally winds down to a welcome halt. In a meeting this long, everyone is mentally exhausted and unable to function at the most productive level.

It may take courage but the only way to put a stop to long, unproductive meetings is to set a maximum meeting length and then to take the steps necessary to stay within that maximum. What is a reasonable maximum for a typical board or committee meeting?

Try a little experiment. The next time you are in a seemingly endless meeting, watch the time as you observe the other participants. Almost invariably you'll find that when the meeting has been going for about an hour-and-a-half it effectively breaks down in one way or another.

This breakdown may take any of several forms. Most often it is shown because the members have become restless and easily distracted. Even those who have until then kept their minds strictly on the meeting's business, begin to make little jokes, or to talk about their plans for the weekend, or even to check their email or begin texting. Some members will become touchy and argumentative. Others will retreat into their shells and cease participating altogether, with their facial expressions and body language showing that they are feeling impatient and grumpy. Whatever the form of the breakdown, somewhere near the 90-minute mark, what has earlier been a productive meeting has been transformed into an entirely different, and unsatisfactory, gathering of distracted people.

It's almost as if the human attention span has a stop button set for 90 minutes.

What does this tell us about our meetings? If at all possible, we should design them so they run for no more than 90 minutes. And you may be surprised to find that it is almost always possible to do so.

(The only exception would be a gathering that is more of a *retreat* or an *information session* or a *workshop* that isn't a decision-making meeting like those that are the primary focus of this book. Even for such sessions, to avoid participant fatigue the schedule should provide for 30-to-60 minute breaks at least every 90 minutes.)

We start the move toward time management by setting the closing time for the meeting at exactly 90 minutes after the time for opening it.

The organizations that have set a 90-minute limit on their meeting length have almost invariably found that at least as much productive work is done in the shorter period as in the former meetings that were much longer. The limit on total meeting time not only keeps the meeting shorter, but it tends to make it more effective and productive.

When all of the participants know the allotted time limit is hovering in the background, this has a marked effect on the discussion during the meeting. The participants, often unconsciously, tend to keep their comments shorter and more to the point. This makes it easier for the other participants to follow the discussion, because there is less said that is unrelated to the topic of the moment.

This contrasts with the different meeting atmosphere that exists when it is assumed that the meeting can drift on as long as necessary, so there is no pressure to keep discussion from wandering. When this time pressure is lacking, discussion *does* wander and become garbled, making it more difficult for the participants to follow it.

As an added bonus, when the participants know in advance that they can plan on the meeting being finished at a fixed time, they don't feel that it is as much of an intrusion in their personal lives, so they are more willing to attend.

But, someone is sure to say, "We'd like to have shorter meetings but we have a lot of work to do. How can we get it all done in ninety minutes?" The answer is that you allocate specific times to the various parts of the agenda, keeping the total time allocated within the agreed 90-minute total.

But the real question is: How do you know how much time to allocate to each agenda item?

You start with a handful of items that will appear in every agenda, month after month. As you will see, for these items it is easy to *know* how much time to allocate to them.

Estimating times needed for the routine procedural items

With a little thought and some experience you can estimate with remarkable accuracy how long will be needed for each agenda item. Also, any time that is allocated for one topic but not fully needed is available to cover a slight over-run for another topic, so the overall meeting time remains within the established limit.

You can easily and accurately estimate the time that will be required for each of the opening items.

It takes only a few seconds to call the meeting to order and to state that a quorum is present. The agenda and the previous meeting's minutes will have been distributed to the participants a few days before the meeting so everyone will have had opportunity to consider them and raise questions if they wish to do so. Because of this they are ideally suited for approval by unanimous consent, which makes it easy to know how much time they will need.

For a practical test you start by writing out the words you would use to cover these items in the meeting. You will come up with something like the words that follow.

> "The meeting will come to order. A quorum is present; proper notice was given. The agenda was distributed before the meeting and there were no questions, so if there are no objections now, [*pause for 2-3 seconds*] the agenda is approved by unanimous consent. The minutes of the previous meeting were also distributed in advance. If there are no corrections now, [*pause*] the minutes are approved by unanimous consent. The first item for discussion is..."

Keeping track of the time, read aloud (to yourself) the words you have written for this opening of the meeting, using the same pace you would use to say them during the meeting.

You will find that they take less than one minute. (It's amazing how much can be said in what seems like a very short time.)

You allot one minute on the agenda for these preliminary routine items.

If there is a Consent Register it is something for which approval by unanimous consent is also advisable, because the real approval has already taken place by the person recommending approval, and again no participant has objected to any of the topics included in it.

So you allot one more minute to formal acknowledgment and approval by consent of the Consent Register. You won't need the full minute, but it might seem a bit over the top to allot only part of a minute.

Providing for the closing steps

Before allocating times for the main topics, we have to decide how much time to reserve for two other essential steps that will appear in the closing minutes of the meeting. They are the line "Items Received Too Late for the Agenda" and the one that allows for confirming or arranging for the next meeting. How much time will these items need?

One of the best ways to answer this question is to watch the time that is actually used in a typical board meeting to discuss an average topic. As long as the discussion has remained focused on the topic itself, you will probably find that for the average topic, by eight minutes everything relevant has already been said at least once and the group could come to a decision without feeling constrained.

Based on this observation, it is reasonable to allot eight minutes to the line for "Items Too Late...." This time allotment should allow for an average topic to be brought up, discussed, and decided.

Then comes the item labeled, "Next meeting." If the time and place remain the same from month to month, all that is needed is to refer to them in a few words. Still, it is useful to keep this line in the agenda as a reminder to everyone.

Highlighting them in this way encourages participants to check their calendars, so they can warn everyone if they will have a conflict and will be unable to attend the next meeting. It is also helpful for everyone to look ahead and make sure that the next scheduled date doesn't conflict with a holiday or an event that might make it advisable to move to another meeting place or date or time.

If you do have to find a new date or time, it is much easier to arrange it cooperatively while the members are all together and can discuss it, than after they have gone home and you have to communicate with them individually.

The final item is, not surprisingly, adjournment. It may seem unnecessary to include this as a line in the agenda. But in the flurry of wrapping up business and getting ready to leave, it is easy for the chair to neglect to say the few words needed to adjourn the meeting. Without those words, it may be unclear when the meeting is officially over. Then you might be faced with misunderstandings as to whether something happened during the meeting and is therefore official, or immediately afterwards and so was not part of the meeting. Having the line on the agenda reminds you to actively declare the meeting adjourned.

Two minutes will usually be ample for confirming or setting the next meeting time and place and for the chair's announcement that the meeting is adjourned.

Now we have completed the allocation of times for the essential steps that have to be part of the meeting, but don't require extended discussion. We have managed to compress to a relatively small total of 13 minutes the combination of the allocations for the routine procedural items, for approval of the Consent Register, for Items Too Late..., and for the closing items. This leaves 77 minutes (out of the 90-minute maximum).

By controlling the time to be spent on items that don't require extended discussion, we have arranged for the meeting to truly focus on its fundamental purpose – *discussion and decision about the main topics*. (Does this last term sound familiar? It has been repeated several times and will be again, because it represents the purpose that we want to keep foremost in our minds as we plan and conduct the meeting.)

Your next task is to divide the remaining uncommitted minutes among the main topics, making sure that for each topic enough time is available for full and open discussion.

Timing the main topics

Scholars who study learning theory tell us that in a relatively small group such as a board or committee, before discussion of even a complicated topic reaches the 20-minute mark, participants have begun to let their concentration drift away.[2] How, then, can the meeting focus be kept on the topics that are to be discussed and decisions made about them?

The key is to make sure that each topic is defined so that it requires only 20 minutes or less, so the introduction of the topic that follows it refreshes the participants' attention.

But will it limit discussion too much to stay within less than the 20-minute maximum?

"There's no way we can come to a decision, the meeting has only lasted half an hour."

Over the years I have observed, as I suspect that you have, that in a serious discussion about a topic almost all productive comments are put forward in the first few minutes. Thereafter most comments repeat

2 Statistics Brain Research Institute."Attention Span Statistics." April 2, 2015.

Wilson, K. and Korn, J.H. "Attention during lectures: Beyond ten minutes." *Teaching of Psychology* 34, no. 2 (2007):85-89.

what has already been said, although perhaps in different words and by different people. Since little is gained from simple repetition, there is little reason to let it take up meeting time.

Perhaps surprisingly, as long as discussion is kept focused on the subject matter, eight minutes seems to be a reasonable amount of time needed for discussion of and decision about an average topic. (Chapters 7 and 8 describe a number of methods the chair can use to help keep discussion focused.)

You work with the draft of the agenda that has the major topics listed, using the wording you have decided on and placed in the order you have selected.

As noted above, the first major topic starts two minutes after the call to order. For the amount of time to allot for it, try starting with eight minutes, and varying it upward or downward depending on several factors, including:

- ✓ the variety of possible solutions for the topic;
- ✓ the topic's complexity;
- ✓ the cost or scope of possible solutions; and
- ✓ the extent to which participants may be personally invested in specific outcomes.

The end of the time for the first topic becomes the starting time for the second topic. And so on, through the major topics, one-by-one, allowing the amount of time for each that you estimate it will require.

When you have gone through all of the major topics, you see whether completion of the last one would leave the required 10 minutes (8 + 2) needed for the line item "Items Too Late..." plus the two closing items.

If the time in this first cut has gone beyond the 90-minute limit you will have to adjust the individual topic times to bring the total down.

Fitting the individual times within 90 minutes

Ways that will allow you to make the needed adjustment may include:

- ✓ re-thinking the individual amounts of time you have set for the major topics;
- ✓ dividing large topics into smaller sub-topics; or
- ✓ removing a topic for later decision or for decision by a subsidiary group.

We'll discuss each of these general possibilities in turn.

Rethinking the tentative allotments

Think about what *needs* to be said about each topic, allowing for fresh ideas and disagreement, and for reaching consensus and decision. Then scale down the amount of time you have allotted for each topic proportionate to the factors that apply to it and keeping in mind the remarkable number of words that can be said in the space of a single minute.

With careful analysis you will probably be able to bring the total allotment for all of the major topics to within the cut-off time.

If the total still brings the final major discussion past the 80-minute mark, to bring it down further you go to the second possible way to adjust the times.

Sub-dividing the main topics

It is often possible to reduce the time needed to cover a topic thoroughly, by dividing it into smaller subtopics.

It might seem that splitting a topic into subtopics would add to the overall time required to discuss it. On the contrary, often the total time required for the total of all of the subtopics individually is less than would have been required for the basic topic if it had been taken as a whole. How can this be?

To explain this apparent paradox, let's assume that the board is considering whether to hold a public forum to publicize one of its projects. During discussion, one participant suggests a couple of appropriate panelists; the next participant refers to the need for adequate publicity; the third questions the cost. Only then a fourth participant comes back to the question of panelists. This large, comprehensive topic causes discussion to be fragmented, jumping from subtopic to subtopic. This scattering of attention can lead to confusion and is time consuming.

If each of these subtopics were to be a separate line on the agenda, discussion at any moment would be focused on a single subtopic. It would be resolved before the next subtopic was addressed, making it easier for everyone to follow what is being said and to respond. The result of the subdivision is that the combined times spent on three subtopics is less than what would have been required if all three had been up for discussion at the same time.

If subdividing topics doesn't bring all of the major ones within the total available time, there is still one step available to you – to remove some of the topics.

Removing a topic or some subtopics from the agenda

It should probably be up to the board to decide whether to hold or not hold such a public forum. Then, if the board decides that a forum should take place, it would be practical to assign to a committee or special task force the details of planning for and conduct of the forum. These details need not take up the board's meeting time.

In addition, by giving the listed topics a second look, you may be able to identify one or more for which decisions could properly be made by an officer or by some other group, especially if guidelines are provided for them. Deciding on the guidelines might be less time-consuming than for the board to discuss and reach agreement on details of the topic itself.

Furthermore, once the board has established guidelines within which similar decisions can be made by others, the board is relieved of the burden of making parallel decisions every time the situation repeats itself.

As a last resort, there might also be a topic or two that could be postponed to the next meeting as long as the delay doesn't cause serious damage.

In the unlikely event that none of these possibilities brings the agenda within the planned working time, this might be an indication that the board has taken responsibility for too much operational detail that should be handled elsewhere. If so, it has been keeping the board from concentrating on broader policy and strategic questions.

On the other hand, if thorough analysis shows that the board is the proper place for all of these decisions, perhaps it will have to meet more frequently until it has cleared the accumulated backlog.

Whatever the possible solutions to the time squeeze, what we know about meeting length tells us that extending it beyond 90 minutes would be counterproductive. It wouldn't be a solution; it would just create different problems.

We have completed the allocations of time. We are ready to put everything into action, which is the subject of the next chapter.

Chapter 5

Getting Ready

Having invited input from the participants, you have selected which major topics will be included; you have decided on their wording and the order in which they will be taken up for discussion; you have estimated the times that will be needed for each topic and segment of the meeting; and you have designed the agenda to shape the meeting. You are almost ready to go to the meeting, but there are a few more preliminary actions that are necessary to complete the pre-meeting process.

Providing pre-meeting materials

It is important to provide the participants with copies of the agenda a few days prior to the meeting. This serves as a reminder of the meeting date and also that the meeting *will start* at the specified time. It also reminds the participants of the major topics that will be discussed so they will be thinking about them in advance and be able to come to the meeting prepared to discuss them.

The minutes of the previous meeting will need to be approved. For the participants to have read them and made sure they are correct in every respect, they too have to be in the participants' hands several days before the meeting at which they will be approved.

If there is to be a Consent Register, its final draft also has to be provided to the participants well before the meeting.

The same is true for any background material that has been gathered for the participants' information and understanding. It doesn't matter whether the group is large or small, volunteer or commercial, board, committee, or a group of colleagues, handing out written material at the beginning of a meeting is worse than a waste of time.

It is natural to assume that if material is handed to the participants, they will read and understand it. Yet, those attending a meeting are eager to get on with its business. So usually the time allowed for reading material is not enough for even the fastest readers and certainly not enough for those who read more deliberately.

If different participants have covered different amounts of the material handed out during the meeting, this defeats the purpose of having that material available to them. Some participants will have picked up some of the information, others will have picked up other information and no one will have absorbed everything that was in the written material. So providing the material has failed in its purpose--that is, to have all participants start from the same base of information.

An experience from my distant past illustrates how ineffective it can be to hand out material during the meeting, as well as how this fact was brought home to me.

The serious disadvantages of handing out written or financial information at a meeting are not cured by using Power Point, Keystone, or any other software, to project material on a screen. Whatever method is used, the participants will not fully grasp it, and it will come too late to be of much use.

MAKING A POINT

Early in my professional career I was elected to the board of directors of an old, traditional insurance company. I soon discovered that every monthly board meeting followed the same pattern. As soon as we directors arrived, each of us was handed a beautifully bound, multi-page report of company operations for the past month plus management's proposals for the next period. The CEO always invited us to "take a few minutes to read your meeting binder."

Although I was a fast reader, I never had time to finish the whole report before the CEO called the meeting to order. Throughout the meeting, senior managers would make proposals and the board would vote on them. Each time I felt uneasy because I knew I didn't have enough information to make an informed decision. But the board was expected to "decide" so I made a guess, crossed my fingers, and voted. I was uncomfortable, but this was my first experience as a company director, and being young and inexperienced I assumed that this must be how boards always functioned.

After my first three months on the board, the CEO retired as had been planned. He was replaced by Jack Hodgkins, whom I knew and who had recruited me to the board. Out of my respect for Jack I had great expectations for positive change.

I was deeply disappointed when Jack's first board meeting started the same way as always before. We were handed the same leather-covered binders; we were offered a few minutes to try to read them.

The most important matter in this report was the description of a new tax amendment that might cost the company several million dollars. When Jack called the meeting to order this topic was, of course, the subject of considerable discussion.

After a few minutes of concerned discussion Jack asked us what we thought about the new tax's effect on directors. We directors looked blankly at each other, since not one of us had caught anything about directors in our hurried reading. Jack called our attention to a sentence in the middle of one of the pages that was analyzing the effects of the change in taxes. It read: *"The individual directors will be required to contribute personally the amount of the company's additional tax liability."*

There was dead silence for a moment. Then we saw the big grin that was spreading across Jack's face, and we realized that he had spoofed us. Of course the suggestion was ridiculous - just as it was ridiculous to have been expecting us to read and digest many pages of highly technical information in a few minutes.

Jack had made his point dramatically. We discussed what to do about the situation. We agreed that thereafter on the Saturday, before the regular monthly meeting which was always held on the third Thursday, a company courier (this being before the age of computers) would deliver to the home of each of the directors, the full meeting binder. It was still bound in beautiful red leather, with each individual copy having the respective director's name embossed in gold on the front cover. But its timing made it completely different from what had been the past practice.

Having it in our hands five days before the meeting gave us each time to read it thoroughly and thoughtfully. Then when we came to the meeting we were prepared to discuss and actually *decide* the issues that were before us.

We appreciated the crucial change that Jack had engineered, but to get back at him for having made us look rather silly, we demanded that he treat us all to a nice dinner after the next board meeting.

But there remains the question: *When* should background information, reports, the agenda, (and the Consent Register if there is to be one), be given to the participants?

If the material is distributed too long before the meeting the participants are likely to say to themselves, "I'll put this aside and read it when I have more time." Then they, being human, are likely to forget and never got around to reading it.

On the other hand, if they receive it too close to the meeting, they may not have time to study it, which defeats the purpose of having produced it.

For board or committee meetings that are held once a month, some organizations have settled on five days before the meeting as the optimum time to distribute material. But the best way to make this decision is to ask the participants and to have them decide! After a few months' trial with whatever timing they choose, you can raise the question again and see if the timing should be adjusted in the light of experience.

The important thing is that you agree as a group when to distribute the pre-meeting material and then, *without fail,* to meet that deadline every month.

It would not be surprising if someone who was responsible for preparing some pre-meeting material would occasionally miss the announced deadline. If you send it out late you are almost inviting people to disregard the deadline in the future. If you allow this, soon no one will feel any obligation to complete their work on time.

So, if something is late, the only safe response is to say, "We have made a promise to ourselves that we won't drop things on each other at the last minute. Thank you for your report. It missed this meeting, and will go out to the board members with the package for the *following* meeting."

Note that it is softer to say that the *report* missed the deadline, than that the *person* who prepared it did so. Just another way to make a point without seeming to be too critical.

You may find that in your first few meetings as chair, some of the participants will not have read more than a portion of the material that was distributed in advance. You can encourage them to complete their pre-meeting reading by keeping the material relatively brief. It can be compressed in summaries, by using point form, or perhaps by using charts and graphs for information that lends itself to these forms. And over time, by using the chairing techniques described in Chapter 7, you can encourage the participants to accept their unspoken but important commitment to read the material in advance.

Creating a productive and pleasant atmosphere

As has been pointed out, your mood and positive manner as chair will help to create a pleasant and collaborative atmosphere before, during, and after the meeting. There are also other steps that can be taken in advance to help in this respect.

With this in mind some chairs arrange for coffee and tea and perhaps snacks, to be available before and during the meeting. There is no doubt that this may help to create a social atmosphere, but is this the mood in which a meeting will be most productive?

If social beverages are to be available at the beginning of the meeting this usually means that someone will be fussing with arrangements, either delaying the call to order, or even missing the first few minutes of the meeting. Besides, if people are busy during the meeting with refilling cups and passing cookies, they are personally distracted and they distract everyone else from the business of the meeting.

Another approach, which has worked well in a number of organizations, is always to have arranged for a social time *immediately following* the meeting. This doesn't interfere with the meeting. But it lets members decompress from any tensions that might have risen during the meeting, and then be free to enjoy each other's company. Most participants look forward to such social contacts, and are willing to postpone them until after the meeting is adjourned. And it doesn't prevent anyone who has another pressing commitment from hustling away immediately after the meeting is adjourned, so the group will have kept its commitment to keep the meeting to no more than 90 minutes.

Choosing the time to meet

A board may almost always have met at the same time and place. When it is time to elect new members of the board, however, it is useful to have a brief meeting with all of the continuing and the new members combined to settle on the time of day and perhaps the day of the month that will be most convenient for most members.

There is no magic time that will suit everyone. But the important thing is for you to find out what most of the continuing and the in-coming members would prefer.

A daytime meeting may effectively exclude some people whose working hours are fixed; an evening meeting may exclude some older people who are not comfortable with being out at night or with driving after dark. An evening meeting may also be relatively unproductive and even tend to being argumentative, because some participants are tired after a long work day and are not as flexible as they might otherwise have been.

To make meetings available to both of these possible groups, you might suggest trying meetings on a weekend. Of course, this timing might eliminate some potential members who reserve weekends for religious obligations or for family times.

And you shouldn't overlook the possibility of breakfast meetings. Unlike an evening meeting, when participants are tired, at breakfast they are likely to be fresh. Some may welcome the opportunity to take care of their board responsibilities before they dive into the busyness of the day. Others may be totally put off by even the thought of an early start. The important thing is to meet the preferences of as many of the group as possible.

ONE WAY TO KEEP MEETINGS SHORT

A friend recently mentioned to me how much she gets from her attendance at weekly meetings of several dozen fellow downtown-business owners. She said that every week a different member describes the goals, the problems, and the rewards, of that person's business. Then there is an open mic for everyone to share tips and concerns that might be of interest to other members.

> My own experience has been that entrepreneurs are so enthusiastic about their work that they can hold forth about it at great length. So I mused, "The chair must have a tough time keeping the meeting from running too long."
>
> "Oh no, not all. That used to be a problem when we met in the evenings. Now we meet in the morning, starting promptly at 8:00. We eat breakfast as we hold the meeting. At 9:00 we all rush off to our offices and shops to start the business day."

Whatever the group decides, it is best to have dates set well in advance, so each meeting gets on everyone's calendar before some other commitment bumps it.

Finding a neutral meeting place

Where to meet may be another question. The ideal may be at the facilities of the parent organization, as long as it has a room available that has a large table and good lighting, and the meeting can be kept free from interruption.

If this option is not available, it might occur to you to volunteer your home for board meetings. It would be wise, however, to wait and give this a second thought. Throughout everything you do in connection with the meeting you are working hard not only to act neutrally, but also to reinforce the image of your neutrality. Meeting in your home, however, gives the impression that it is *your* meeting.

Besides, if you have to serve as host you will be distracted from your tasks as chair by the need to arrange for enough seating, lighting, and table space, to greet latecomers, and to generally to make sure members' needs are met.

If your home is out, how about the home of another member? It is a fallback choice if necessary but it may not be the best from the standpoint of how it may shape the meeting. A home is personal and social. It sets the tone of the meeting, making it also personal and social. Yet what works best for a meeting is an atmosphere that is impersonal and businesslike. So it may be better to find a place where the atmosphere is less inviting.

Some libraries, community centers, and even some commercial establishments, offer meeting rooms at no charge for community-oriented organizations. Meeting in such an impersonal location tends to set the tone as one in which the focus is on the business at hand – exactly what you are looking for.

It is worth taking some time to explore these possibilities, but you may still have to meet in members' homes. In that case, you will want to arrange to take turns on a rotation amongst the members instead of always going to the same one.

Making final preparations

You will want to organize your papers for the meeting. It's always a good idea to do this a day or so in advance. This gives you time to work around any glitches that you couldn't correct if they had surfaced at the last moment. Printers have a way of breaking down when you are short of time, copies of crucial documents lose themselves and can't be found, keys hide in unexpected places, and traffic jams appear out of nowhere just as you are driving to the meeting place. Murphy's Law tells us that if something can go wrong, it will. So give yourself the extra time to foil Murphy.

What do you want to take to the meeting? Your check list might look something like this:

- ✓ Enough copies of the agenda for everyone;
- ✓ *One* copy of any document that has recommendations that will be discussed;
- ✓ Your own copy of the current financial report;
- ✓ *One* copy of every other document that was distributed before the meeting;

- ✓ A watch or other readily visible device that shows the correct time;
- ✓ A list of the names and contact numbers of the members and possibly of others whom you might unexpectedly need to reach; and
- ✓ A pen and pad.

As for the agenda copies, some members will bring the agenda they received a few days earlier, but there are probably others who will not. Even if the participants have the agenda on a tablet or on another device, you surely want an agenda copy in front of each member, staring right up at them so they are kept constantly aware of the times suggested on it.

Sometimes a document that has been distributed in advance will include a recommendation that requires discussion and decision. In that case, the *recommendation*, but not the report or other document, will be on the agenda for discussion and decision. In this way you have focused on the issue that needs attention, without allowing the discussion to wander off into other aspects of the document, undoing some of the benefits of having distributed it in advance.

Still, as a precaution, it may be useful to have a copy of the whole document in case during the discussion it becomes desirable to check some detail in it. But unless you need to refer to it during discussion, this document will remain tucked away in your briefcase unless and until you bring it out for a particular purpose.

Contact lists will probably not be needed at most meetings. Even so, it is frustrating not to be able to get in touch with someone if it seems desirable in the moments immediately after the meeting adjourns, while the members are still nearby and can participate in the contact.

Of course, you will need to be able to keep track of the time throughout the meeting. At some points during discussion you may want quietly to emphasize the passing of time. Then you can make a point of looking at the time in an obvious manner. When you do so, the participants are likely to react in much the same way as if you had orally pointed out the need to get on with the business. But in this way, the group discipline as to time will be coming from them rather than with pressure from you.

At other times you may want to check the time without creating any unspoken "hurry-up" suggestion. Yet you may be sure that the participants will be constantly observing you as their chair, so almost anything you do will have some effect on them, whether intentional or not. So you will want to be able to check the time by a simple glance that is not noticed. A watch on the table beside you will allow you to do this less obtrusively than if you have to re-awaken a hand-held device that has gone into sleep mode.

And the pen and pad? Not necessary if you have a perfect memory in all things and at all times. On the other hand, if you are only human, you will find it very helpful to make various brief notes during the meeting. Like checking the time, making a brief handwritten note is less obtrusive and attracts less attention than tapping at a keyboard of any type.

Of course, if the meeting participants are all techies, using a pen may identify you as a throwback to the Stone Age, so you may wish to follow the herd and avoid any tool that is not electronic.

As you organize the items you will take, it is always a good idea to glance through the agenda once again, to make sure that you have thought of everything that you might need during the meeting.

Arriving early

Now you are ready to head off to the meeting. Since you will be setting the pattern for the other participants it is essential for you to arrive well before the scheduled meeting time. If the meeting place is some distance from your home (or from your office if that is where you are starting from) you will have to allow what may seem like too much time in order to allow for any unexpected delay.

Remember that it is not enough to say, "I am late because traffic was backed up." What that really means is, "I am late because I didn't leave home early enough to allow for a traffic backup." And if you are late, you may be sure that others will relax and decide that it isn't really very important to have meetings start and end on time.

To allow for the unexpected – some of which is almost sure to confront you – you have to arrive at the meeting room, having parked, disposed of outer wraps, and chosen your seat, an absolute minimum of 10 minutes before the meeting is to begin.

"Sorry I'm late, I've just finished reading this report on punctuality."

If you are going to be using any form of electronic projection or amplification, this lead time probably should be up to a full hour, to allow you to make whatever adjustments you will need to make, so they don't crop up at the moment when you depend upon the equipment.

Whatever timing you choose for a particular meeting, you must clear your schedules for other matters sufficiently early that you won't be embarrassed and undo all of your work to start and end meetings on time.

A LUCKY ESCAPE

Several years ago I was asked to serve as chair of the governing board of a church of which I was a new member. I was warned that its meetings were always scheduled to start at 7:00 but would not really begin until nearly 7:30. Then they had always extended late into the evening, often becoming so tense that members sometimes came close to fisticuffs. No one was taking any steps to make better use of meeting time.

As the first step in improving the meetings I made as a condition of my acceptance of the chairmanship that meetings would start and finish at exactly the times that were announced for them. The two men who were trying to recruit me as chair smiled in a patronizing manner, with one saying, "Well, you can try."

For my first three monthly meetings I was absolutely insistent on both starting and adjourning at precisely the scheduled times, regardless of how many members were late for the opening, or what was being discussed at the time for adjournment. Perhaps somewhat encouraged by the new meeting discipline, some of the animosities amongst the members seemed to be softening. I thought I was beginning to make some progress.

Then after dinner one hot August evening I was sitting at the desk in my study, clad only in shorts, and literally sweating over notes for a lecture I was scheduled to give the next day. The phone rang. I almost disregarded it to avoid being interrupted.

Reluctantly, though, I picked up the phone and heard, "Bruce, this is Dave. We had an emergency here at the lab and I haven't been able to get away till this moment. I'll be half an hour late for the meeting. I'm so sorry."

Oops, I thought. *There's a board meeting tonight at 8:00 and that's only ten minutes from now.* I jumped into some clothes, grabbed my briefcase (which fortunately I had packed the day before) and ran – yes, ran – the two blocks to the church, where the meeting was to be held.

I rushed into the boardroom just as the antique mantel clock struck eight. Without waiting to catch my breath I said, "The meeting will come to order. A quorum is present..." and continued with the agenda.

Everyone looked a little startled, but they had the grace not to say anything. After the meeting I explained what had happened and we all had a good laugh. Dave's phone call had saved me from considerable embarrassment. It had also saved the board from possibly lapsing once again into a complete disregard of the need to make productive use of everyone's time.

Preparing mentally by asking, "Why are we having this meeting"?

Just one last mental adjustment. Before you pick up your briefcase and go out is a good moment to sit back and think of why the meeting is being held. The organization's bylaws or the governing law may require that a certain number of meetings be held within a given year. But these requirements could be met technically by merely giving the required notice for the meeting, calling it to order, and adjourning it. The meeting would technically have been held to fulfill the requirements. So there must be other reasons for which you are planning to hold the meeting.

And indeed there are other reasons. The meeting will take place because there are decisions that need to be made and a meeting is the appropriate place to make them. How will these decisions be arrived at? By the members exchanging ideas and then reaching agreement among themselves. In other words, by discussion – the reason to have people get together for a meeting.

So as you head out to serve as chair you say to yourself, almost as a mantra: "My objective is to facilitate, manage, and mentor the participants so they will collaboratively arrive at the best informed decisions they can possibly make in the present circumstances. For 90 minutes, everything I do, every word I say, will be pointed to this objective."

And then to say to yourself very firmly, "It will be an enjoyable, productive meeting, and the participants will be glad to have taken part, and will be pleased with the results."

This may sound like a trivial formula, but I have found that reminding myself of these two points has helped me to keep the balance and the good will that I have sometimes needed in chairing a meeting.

Now, you are prepared, mentally and in all other ways, to make your best contribution during the meeting itself, which we take up in the next chapter.

Chapter 6

Opening The Meeting

You are now almost fully prepared for the meeting itself. You have made sure that the most important major topics will be handled, that they will be worded in such a way as to encourage wide-ranging discussion, and that they are in an order that may help to keep discussion open and productive. You have made sure that background information has been in the hands of the participants in time for them to have read and grasped it; you have carefully designed and distributed an agenda that will serve as a roadmap for the meeting; and you have proposed an appropriate time schedule so that the business of the meeting will be done within a reasonable time. Now you are ready to conduct the meeting as its chair.

Still, there is one other way in which you may find it useful to prepare.

Setting the meeting mood

From your experience you know that every meeting seems to have a somewhat different mood. We've all seen meetings in which the business is disposed of pleasantly and promptly, and others in which everything and everyone seemed to have turned sour.

Often this negative meeting mood developed because of something that happened during the meeting – an unpleasant personal comment, a misunderstanding, even a minor disagreement that escalated. As an alert chair you can usually recognize this development, and take steps to correct it.

All too often, though, you may feel that the atmosphere is tense but you don't know why. It may have resulted from some situation outside the meeting. Maybe one of the participants has had a bad day and feels generally grumpy. Maybe someone has personal concerns about health, finances, or relationships. Maybe two participants have had a minor, or a major, falling out. Whatever the unknown reason, it has been brought into the meeting and affects its atmosphere, making it more difficult to proceed effectively.

There is usually little that you, as chair, can do directly about such unexplained external causes. But, as was pointed out in Chapter 2, you can still set the stage by how you appear to the participants throughout the meeting. If you manage to appear calm, self-controlled (but not controlling), and pleasant, it will do much to quell any negative influences that otherwise might tend to keep the meeting from being at its best. Your own mood may help to save the meeting from being captured by the bad mood or the personal concerns of one or two participants.

Some chairs have found that it helps them to maintain the calm and poise that will be needed during the meeting if, before they set out for the meeting place, they intentionally schedule an uninterrupted 10-minute break in which they sit quietly with a clear mind and a positive outlook. You may find that such an intentional pause in the day's pressures is a useful lead up to the 90 minutes you will be concentrating fully on the meeting.

And now you are fully prepared, and it's off to the meeting.

Getting a head start

Arriving at the meeting place at least 10 minutes early lets you choose your seat. If the table is rectangular or oval, the best place for the chair is at the end opposite the door. Sitting at the end of the table, rather than at its side, gives you an unobstructed view of the members so you can see when they are looking bored, distracted, or grumpy, and take whatever steps may be needed to correct the situation before it is caught by other participants.

If the meeting takes place during daylight hours and your first choice of seat means that you will be facing a window, then it is best to shade the window or to choose your place at the other end of the table. You don't want to find yourself partially blinded by bright light, wreathing the members' faces in halos. Much better to see their expressions and to let them earn their halos in other ways.

When you've chosen your seat, without making a big deal of it you drop your attaché case on the table at that place. No one is likely to pay much attention or to challenge your choice.

You count the chairs, and make sure that there is one for each participant who is expected to attend. If there are more than enough, you remove the extra ones. You don't want an empty seat to appear to invite a visitor to join the participants at the table and join in the board's discussion.

You quickly place one copy of the agenda on the table at each participant s place. Then you sit in your place and take out your copy of any documents whose recommendations will be discussed, arranging them in the order they will come before the meeting.

Sitting down serves as an alert to the members that it's time for them to start settling down as well, so the meeting can get started right on time.

You place your timer beside your agenda, and sit back to calm your mind for the meeting ahead.

There will be three main segments of the meeting, with each handled differently from the others. They are:

- The three or four routine initial items, that usually will not require discussion;
- The main topics, for which discussion is the main reason for the meeting; and
- The three "closing" items that may or may not require brief discussion.

As explained in Chapter 4, the first and third segments use up as little time as possible for whatever needs to be done with them, in order to save time for extended discussion of the middle group – the major topics for which the meeting is called.

Giving the two-minute warning

Meeting time is approaching. If the meeting is set for 7:00, precisely (!) at 6:58, you interrupt whatever may be happening, and announce, "It's 6:58. The meeting will begin in two minutes, so please take your seats so we can start on time."

All too often, right at this moment you will find some member wanting to engage you in conversation. If you allow yourself to be distracted in this way, you are likely to find that in order to respond, you will have to delay starting the meeting – a definite No-No.

If the attempt at conversation seems to be about a topic that is on the agenda, your response is easy. Something like: "Let's wait to discuss this when everyone is able to take part."

If it is about some other topic, you can say, "Sorry, my mind is focused on the meeting that will be starting right away. Let's discuss this after the meeting. Please do remind me of it then."

It is important to put the responsibility back on the other person to raise the question later. In your 90 minutes of concentrated work chairing the meeting, you are unlikely to remember to come back to the matter that you deferred. And you don't want to have it appear that you were just intentionally putting it off so you didn't have to deal with it.

Precisely at 7:00, whatever else may be happening, you say: "It's 7:00 o'clock. The meeting will come to order. A quorum is present. (*And without even stopping for breath…*) "The first item of business is to approve the agenda…."And you proceed with the meeting.

Acknowledging the quorum

The organization's bylaws or the governing laws probably state how many members of the board are needed for a quorum. If they do not, the number for a board is a majority – that is more than half of its members.

"I've called this meeting to discuss absenteeism."

This may not be a problem for a small board or committee meeting, but it may be difficult for a general meeting of the members. Unless the agenda includes an especially interesting or controversial topic, many members of a large organization just do not bother to attend a general meeting. Because of this, it may be desirable to include in the bylaws a figure that is less than half for the quorum for general meetings of members.

The purpose of a quorum requirement is to make sure that enough members are present (or represented by proxy if allowed) so that when decisions are made, they actually reflect the wishes of a representative group of those entitled to vote.

To avoid any question being raised later, it is a good idea for the chair to say the few words needed to state that a quorum is present, and for the minutes to reflect that statement.

Limiting action if a quorum is not present

If a board finds that its regularly scheduled meetings do not attract a quorum of its members, this is a serious reflection on the effectiveness and dedication of its members. This situation requires attention that is wider than the question of a quorum and is beyond the scope of this book.

What if as the meeting time approaches you look around the room and see that there are not enough voting members to meet the quorum requirement? In order to protect the rights of those who are absent, the only business permitted in a meeting that lacks a quorum is:

- ✓ calling the meeting to order;
- ✓ calling a short recess to try to attract enough other members to meet the quorum;
- ✓ setting a date and time to which to adjourn the meeting; and
- ✓ adjourning.

Any other actions are not valid both according to parliamentary rules and to general law.

If you see that the lack of a quorum is only because some participants whom you expect to attend have not yet arrived, there is little that you can do except to wait for them. As soon as they step foot in the room, without waiting for them even to sit down, you immediately say, "The meeting will come to order. We now have a quorum."

Without saying so, you have made clear that all of the other participants have had to wait for the latecomers. It will often be enough of a reminder and a small embarrassment to encourage them to arrive on time for future meetings.

The situation is different in a large meeting of members. Some bylaws provide that if a scheduled meeting of the members does not have a quorum, it can be adjourned to the same time and place one week later and that at that time whatever number of voting members appear will be sufficient to constitute a quorum.

If the meeting has begun with the necessary quorum but then enough members leave the room so the number present falls below the required quorum, it is the duty of the chair, or of any individual present, to call attention to that fact. Then any further business is subject to the same restrictions as applied when the meeting began without a quorum.

It is worth noting that protection of absent members is such an important concept that any attempt to change or to disregard the stated quorum is invalid, except by a formal change in the bylaw.

Of course, a bylaw amendment cannot solve a problem in the current meeting, but must go through the extended procedure of notice, and presentation and approval at a subsequent general meeting. When any such amendment is made it is important to remember that any new level set for a quorum must not be less than whatever the requirement may be in the governing statute.

UNFORESEEN CONSEQUENCES OF BYPASSING A QUORUM REQUIREMENT

Several years ago I joined a political organization and to my surprise at the next annual general meeting I was elected as a member of the 14-member board. A few days later, the president called an emergency board meeting to take care of an important matter that had come up. As it happened, at the time chosen for the special meeting a violent storm hit the city. I was one of the seven members who braved the rain and wind to reach the meeting place.

The organization's bylaws require a majority of the members of the board to be physically present to constitute a quorum at a special meeting of this type. It was felt that a decision had to be made immediately so corrective action could be taken, but since there wasn't a quorum, we faced a dilemma. The president phoned those of the absent members he could reach to see if they would be attending. None would be doing so.

After some thought, the president came up with a possible solution. There would be no meeting, but those of us present would discuss the emergency problem informally. We would not make any decisions, but we would reach agreement on what the right decision might be if a decision were to be made! Then at the next regularly scheduled board meeting the tentative solution would be presented as a motion, and approved without the necessity for discussion. And in the meantime the emergency would have been resolved.

This seemed like a bizarre approach, but it might work. No one foresaw the possible hazard.

The tentative solution was presented at the next regular meeting of the board. Three of the members who had missed the non-meeting took strong exception to the proposed solution. They convinced several other board members, including some who had agreed originally with the informal solution, that it was unwise. They voted against the proposed motion and defeated it.

As might have been expected, since the situation was an emergency requiring immediate response, some other members had acted on the tentative solution before the regular meeting that had been expected to approve it. Thus, in fact they had taken serious, and as it happened, irreversible action *without*

> *authority.* They and the board members who had acquiesced in the president's seemingly clever stratagem, were severely criticized. The bad will in the board continued for long afterward.
>
> In the circumstances it was difficult to know what might have solved the problem, but the experience showed that trying to bypass a quorum requirement is a hazardous venture.

What do you do if the bylaw or the governing statute requires that a meeting be held within a specified time, and at that time there is no quorum? Fortunately, there is welcome relief. Just having called the meeting to order legally meets that requirement, even though no business can be done at the meeting.

Covering for an absent secretary

Normally a secretary who is unavoidably going to miss a meeting will warn the chair in advance. This gives you time to choose a substitute and to brief that person on the secretary's immediate duties and what to include in the minutes.

If the secretary's absence takes you by surprise, however, you will have to decide what to do on the spur of the moment. It may be tempting for you to take on the role of acting secretary yourself. On second thought, you will probably remember your need as chair to concentrate fully on the progress of the meeting, so you will decide that this is probably not a good solution.

Instead, in most cases, your best solution will be to appoint as acting secretary someone known to be reliable and attentive, and quickly explain the proper scope of the minutes. As a fail-safe practice, in this case it is advisable to ask the person appointed to sit next to you so you can indicate when something is occurring that should be reflected in the minutes.

In this case it is especially important for the chair to review the first draft of the minutes, before they receive wider circulation.

Responding to a latecomer

The first time or two that you are chair, there are likely to be latecomers. When you call the meeting to order, or just before you do, a member will probably say something like, "I saw Peter in the hall, let's wait a minute for him."

You have two options. One is to wait for Peter, and start the meeting two, three, or five minutes late. If you do this, the agenda's suggested timings will all have to be adjusted and time remaining for productive discussion will have been cut.

More important, disregarding the starting time tells the members that time isn't really vey important. This eventually slips into a complete disregard for timing. The participants begin to think that it doesn't matter when the meeting starts, and that it might as well run on until everyone drops from exhaustion. Let's not go there.

Your better option is to say, "It's not fair to those who are here to have to wait for those who haven't been able, for whatever reason, to get here on time. When Peter comes in he can pick up what has happened and go on from there."

By following the second option you have been fair to everyone, including the late member, and you have reinforced the importance of meeting times. As long as Peter comes in within the first five minutes or so, he won't have missed any of the crucial discussion. If he is even later than that it is his problem, not the problem of the other members of the group.

How do you react to members when they arrive late? When they come in you nod pleasantly, but do not interrupt what you or anyone is saying. Nor do you reward the latecomers by trying to recap what has happened in the meeting. It is up to the latecomers to catch up. The rest of the members should not have their time wasted and their concentration broken because someone else was unable (or unprepared) to arrive on time.

Approving the agenda

The agenda is the first item of business after the acknowledgement of the quorum and the call to order. It does not require discussion at this point, because the participants have received it and any questions have been resolved. It is, though, important for the participants actually to approve the agenda. When they do so, they are effectively saying that this is how they want, and expect, the meeting to progress.

So you say something like, "The final agenda was distributed to you on [*Wednesday*?]. The copies before you are identical to those that were distributed [*except* ...]. Does everyone agree to adopt it for this meeting?" [*You pause for perhaps three seconds, as you glance quickly around the members. Then you go on*...] "The agenda is adopted by unanimous consent."

LEARNING FROM MY OMISSION

A number of years ago I was nervous about a board meeting that I was going to chair and that I knew would raise some highly emotional issues. In the moments before it was time to call the meeting to order, despite my attempts to divert them, several participants had already started to argue with their fellow members.

I was frustrated and flustered, and in starting the meeting I neglected to have the agenda approved by the participants. The meeting proceeded, however, as if it had been approved.

Near the end of the meeting a visitor, who was not a member of the board, asked to add a topic that I knew would be explosive, especially since the participants were already feeling somewhat edgy. I responded that the agenda did not allow time for any unplanned business.

The visitor pointed out that the agenda had never been approved by the participants. I realized that she was absolutely right and that, in effect, we did not have an agenda. Therefore, I couldn't rightly say that there was no room for her new topic.

This was long ago and I've forgotten how we resolved this problem. What I *do* remember is how embarrassed I was by my failure to have made sure that the agenda be approved. And I don't think I have ever since failed to make sure that the agenda included a line for its own approval early in the meeting.

Dealing with an unexpected pressure group

If a group of the organization's members want to make a presentation to the board they will usually let you know in advance. Then you can adjust the agenda, or depending on the nature of their presentation, schedule a special meeting to hear their concerns.

If the group failed to alert you sufficiently in advance, you may discover on arriving at the meeting place that they've descended on the board meeting and expect to be heard. Given that they did not exhibit normal courtesy in their failure to alert you to their plans, it is probably because they are functioning from anger and will be insistent that they be given time in the meeting.

If tempers are too high among the visitors you may have to deal with them immediately, or even omit calling the meeting to order and announce that the meeting is rescheduled for another date.

In most cases, you can postpone dealing with them until after the agenda is approved. Having approved the agenda first, does three things. 1) It makes clear that the 90-minute meeting is already scheduled fully; and 2) It helps to recapture for the participants the orderly flow of their meeting; and 3) It establishes the allotted 8-minute slot for Items Received Too Late for the Agenda.

If the members of this pressure group are reasonably accepting, you proceed with calling the meeting to order and asking for approval of the agenda. Then you ask them to state briefly the subject of their concerns.

When they do so, you can pleasantly point out to them that there is a time allotted in the agenda for "Items Received Too Late for the Agenda" and that their topic will be placed there. They may be disgruntled at having to wait, but they have little choice and, in the circumstances, little reason to complain.

It may also serve as an object lesson to them, as they sit through the meeting waiting for their time near the end. They may learn and copy the way in which the participants focus on the topic being discussed and avoid distracting conversation.

When their time comes, it is even more important than usual for you, as chair, to keep control of the meeting, because by the very nature of the situation, feelings are likely to run rather high. Also, the visitors will not be easily kept within the time allotted.

When it seems likely that they will run over the planned time, you can suggest that they choose from among the various possibilities – to describe their concerns to the board in writing, to seek a place on the agenda for the next meeting, or if the issue is one of great urgency, to return to a specially-called meeting of the board.

In the interests of democratic process and also to avoid being seen as the villain in the piece, you put any proposed solution to the board members for a motion and vote. Whatever you do, you do not allow the visitors to force the meeting to go on beyond the originally scheduled time.

Correcting the minutes

Immediately after announcing that the agenda has been approved (either by unanimous consent or by having taken a vote), you go on to say: "The next item is the minutes of the meeting of [*date*]. Are there any corrections?"

There are two things to note about this wording. One is that the question is for *corrections* and not for *approval* of the minutes. The secretary, or someone acting in the secretary's place, has prepared the minutes. That person recorded the actions that were taken and the decisions that were made at the previous meeting. The present board members cannot re-write history by changing the minutes that record what happened. They can only correct any wording that does not accurately reflect what occurred.

The other point to note is that the chair does not ask for "corrections *or additions*."

If a crucial point, such as an approved motion, has been omitted from the minutes, it needs to be inserted. By definition, this addition is a correction so is taken up under that title. But there are other meanings of addition that we want to avoid.

The reason for not saying "additions" is to avoid any invitation to participants to start adding descriptions of bits of discussion that may (or may not) have taken place, but that might appeal to them personally. The secretary (with any approval committee that may be required by the organization's bylaws) has carefully weighed which matters to include in the minutes. The choice between including and not including something has been based on the same criteria, applied consistently. It would create a distortion in the emphasis reflected in the minutes if participants were now to start inserting their own personal preferences in what will become, when approved, the official permanent record.

So, the present board members either adopt the minutes as presented, or correct any errors in them, but they do not start re-writing them.

Unless some question has been raised about the wording of the minutes, they are usually approved by unanimous consent.

(See Chapter 9 for a complete discussion of what should and should not go in minutes.)

Approving the Consent Register

If there is a Consent Register (see Chapter 3) you intend to ask for its approval by unanimous consent in the same way as you did for the agenda, and for the same reasons.

There may be a surprise, however. You will have cleared in advance with the members all of the items on the Consent Register. Even so, when you get to the meeting, a participant may start to comment or raise a question about one of the items on it. On the rare occasion when this occurs, you do not attempt to respond directly. Instead you say, "This item will be removed from the Consent Register and transferred to the agenda section labeled, "Items Received Too Late for the Agenda."

You make a note on your copy of the agenda so you won't forget it and immediately proceed with: "Are there any other items that need to be transferred at this time?" [*After a momentary pause you continue.*]

Because of this unexpected objection to an item that was on the Consent Register, you will want to remove any doubt that the rest of the items on it have been unanimously approved. So, in this occasional situation, to approve the remaining Consent Register it will probably be wise to call for a motion and actual vote by the raising of hands.

Now you've disposed of the routine items and have reached the fun part. Without pausing further you go on to the main purpose of the meeting – discussion of and decisions about the major topics, which is the subject of the next chapter.

Now especially, your skill in chairing the meeting will come into play. And please don't tell yourself that you don't have skills in chairing, because when you apply the suggestions in this book you will have made a good start in developing those special skills.

Not only can you enjoy the meeting, but there will be other rewards as well. Occasionally you will even be surprised by hearing someone say what a great meeting it was – and you'll know it was at least in part because of your work in preparing for the meeting, and in your skill in chairing it.

Chapter 7

The Main Topics for Discussion

You have now arrived at the stage to which much of your careful planning has been directed – the discussion of major topics and the making of decisions about them. As chair you will be exercising all three basic chairing skills – facilitating, managing, and mentoring.

You will keep constantly in mind the need to encourage participation, to be carefully neutral, and to keep the focus of the meeting on the business that is to be done. Your steady hand will keep the meeting on track, unobtrusively and pleasantly.

Facilitating the start of discussion

How you bring up a topic will have a marked effect on the breadth of the discussion about it. To encourage wide-ranging discussion you used a Focus Sentence to select the wording to describe each major topic on the agenda. You don't want unintentionally to undo that good openness by slipping back to what might be a restrictive wording.

In general, to introduce a topic you can just say, "The next item is..." [*and then repeat the exact wording that you had chosen for that item on the agenda*].

Because the participants have known that the topic will come up at the meeting, they will usually be ready to start discussing it. As suggested in Chapter 3, you will have chosen this topic to be first on the agenda because it is relatively simple and non-controversial. If you have guessed right, there should be little delay before someone begins the discussion.

If no one speaks right away, you may have to trigger discussion. You can often do this by asking a simple neutral question such as: "What do we want to do about it?"

A question such as this is useful at any time that discussion of a topic seems to have bogged down, but it is especially helpful early in the meeting when people seem to be hanging back and waiting for others to take the lead.

The question includes the key word that reminds everyone that it is *we* who have to get on with the business of the meeting. This is not a responsibility of the chair alone, nor can it be left to someone else. It is the personal obligation of each participant. And you have made this point without sounding critical.

The question also emphasizes that it is about taking action – that is making decisions, with the added implication that *now* is the time for it.

If this still doesn't stimulate someone to make the first comment on the topic, you may be tempted to start the discussion yourself. If you slip into stating an opinion at this stage, you will be locked into taking a leading part in the discussion that follows. And for the rest of the meeting, you will find yourself having to push aside your responsibilities as chair so that you can think about what you will be saying next. Even the most experienced multi-tasker can't carry on a vital discussion and at the same time pick up on all the nuances involved in chairing.

If you let yourself become front-and-center in the discussion in this way, soon all of the other members will be able to sit back comfortably, and leave most of the discussion's heavy lifting to you.

Instead of falling into this trap, you can use a tool that seldom fails. That tool is *silence*.

Using silence to trigger discussion

For many people in a group, almost anything feels better than experiencing silence. They become very uncomfortable and start to squirm after only a few moments in which no one is speaking. In the busy world we all inhabit, the absence of talk feels unnatural – so unnatural that many people will overcome any hesitancy they may have had about being the first to speak.

To emphasize the artificial silence, you sit perfectly still except for turning your head enough to make eye contact with each participant in turn. You keep a pleasant expression on your face but you say nothing.

It may seem like hours, but a few seconds will probably be enough for this method to work. One of the participants will probably yield to the urge to say something in order to fill the yawning gap caused by silence. What is said at first may not be thought out or very coherent, but the discussion has begun and the awkwardness has been overcome.

You immediately reward the first person who spoke by summarizing in half-a-dozen words the gist of what that person said. Here again, you remain neutral. Whether you agree or disagree with what was said, you restate it accurately, without allowing your own opinions to creep in.

Then you look expectantly to the other participants to continue the discussion. They may agree or disagree with what has been said, or they may disregard it entirely, but the initial hesitancy has been forgotten.

"Going around the table"

Once a discussion has started, it usually continues under its own momentum. But sometimes it comes to a halt for no apparent reason. At this stage, using silence probably won't work as it did at the start of discussion. Once there has been some discussion, silence does not seem so threatening; it just seems only to be a break in the give-and-take.

When faced with lagging discussion, some chairs resort to a method known as "going around the table." Let's see how this works and what its effects can be.

We'll assume that Aaron is immediately to the left of the chair, so in this exercise he is tapped to be the first one to speak. Aaron hasn't yet said anything because so far he hasn't felt he had anything to contribute on this particular subject. But because it is his turn he struggles and comes up with a few words. He has met his obligation to speak, but has added little to discussion of the topic at hand.

Next to Aaron is Bonnie. Going around the table it's now her turn to speak. She is equally at a loss. But she, too, is a good sport and says something in order to do her bit.

Third in the prescribed sequence is Charlie. It happens that while Aaron and Bonnie were filling the air with useless patter, Charlie had an idea. He states it crisply. This triggers new ideas for Aaron and for Bonnie. Both of them would like to respond to Charlie's point. But they can't. They have already had their turns. They can't rudely muscle in and cut out Donna, whose turn is next (because she happens to be sitting at Charlie's left).

And so it goes. In meeting their allotted turns, some participants have to speak before they have anything to say, while at the same time others who may be eager to do so cannot because it is someone else's turn.

Is this the way to stimulate the give-and-take of a productive discussion? Hardly. So what else can you do to kick start a discussion that has faltered?

Unblocking a stalled discussion

One of the best ways to stimulate discussion that seems to have stalled is to summarize what has been said.

Doing so will usually have either of two opposite effects. Sometimes it will emphasize that pretty much everything useful has been said about the topic and that it is time to come to a conclusion.

If the discussion has not jelled, however, a summary may help to bring together the different points of view and point out what is missing.

So, when the chair presents a brief summary, in one case it may hasten arrival at a decision; in another case it may highlight what other concepts need to be raised before the participants are ready to make a decision. In either case it can be a valuable step toward a decision.

It isn't necessary to summarize everything that has been said, but only the high points. You will have to decide which ones to include in your summary, depending on how various participants have reacted to them. Some important points will have led to further discussion, while other points have been accepted without comment, and still others have been ignored as not contributing much to the discussion. It will be up to you to make these distinctions by your close observation of the participants' reactions.

Even if you have the kind of memory for detail that we all wish we had, as discussion bounces along most of your mind's capacity will be directed to what is being said and how various comments fit together or clash with each other.

You ask, "How can I remember all that has been said? I don't want to insult a participant by forgetting what that person has said, if I haven't included it in a summary." The answer is by making brief notes as the discussion goes along.

These notes may be only for your own use, or may be on a flip chart so all participants can see and follow them. Whichever way you make the notes you leave some space so that later similar comments can be added close to the original notes.

Keeping track of discussion

This answer may seem simple, but involves a high degree of judgment, which you will find becomes better with practice.

You won't want to allow your note-taking to distract you from following the course of discussion. If you write notes longer than a few words each, you'll be directing your mind to what you are writing, and you'll miss the next points being made. But if you don't make notes at all, you may have difficulty remembering all of the important points when you summarize.

So the solution is to make *brief* notes – no more than a couple of words for each point – just enough so you can later recall and repeat the various points that have been made.

Your notes will be most useful at two stages. One stage is when you see that the participants are beginning to repeat themselves without adding anything new. No one benefits from allowing meeting time to be taken up by repetition of what everyone has already heard. When you summarize, the participants realize that they are repeating themselves, and that it's time to move forward.

The second stage when a quick summary may be helpful is when discussion is slowing down and doesn't seem to be getting anywhere. You can call attention to the slowdown without seeming to be critical by saying something like, "What I'm hearing you say is…."

These first two reasons for providing a summary may or may not come up in a given discussion. The third reason, however, is almost essential for every major discussion. When the participants are nearing or have actually reached agreement, the chair's summary serves to bring together the concepts that have been suggested. At this point, the summary may be all that is needed to make it possible either to acknowledge agreement by unanimous consent or to welcome a motion and take a vote.

Identifying suggestions with individuals?

As chair you are always thinking of ways to give credit to participants for their contributions to the discussion. So you might refer to an idea that has been presented by describing it as "Tim's suggestion." Or you might ask silent participants, "What do you think of Kayla's idea?"

By naming those who have provided new ideas, you are acknowledging them and indirectly thanking them. Any benefit from this polite recognition, however, may be offset by two disadvantages.

First, everyone's mind tends to wander at times, so some participants may not have heard whatever it was that Tim or Kayla has said, so they cannot comment on it.

Second, naming the person who originated an idea tends to identify that idea with that person. Then it *belongs* to that person, who will feel some obligation to defend it. This locks them into being an advocate for it, and makes it more difficult for them to accept modifications or rejection of it. This creates an atmosphere in which there are two sides, with one side arguing forcefully for the idea, and the other arguing equally forcefully against it. This is the exact opposite of the kind of open, flexible discussion that makes for the most effective meetings.

For both of these reasons, even though it may require a few more words it is much better to identify a comment or suggestion by its content, than by the person who offered it. For example, it is almost as easy, and much better for the course of future discussion, to describe a suggestion that has been made as "The suggestion that we have a public forum..." than to identify it by the name of the person who suggested it.

In this way no one belongs to an idea. It has to stand on its own or be modified or even dropped if that is the will of the group. And no one need feel personally slighted if the group does not act on it.

Using a motion to focus discussion

At some point in the discussion you may sense that participants are zeroing in on a position that is generally acceptable, but that is still rather fuzzy, with different participants having different perceptions of important details. In this situation, a motion may help to clarify matters.

Parliamentary authorities are consistent in saying that in a *large* group it is almost always best if no extensive discussion be permitted until a motion has been made, seconded, and stated by the chair. Then discussion can be directed exclusively to the specific motion or, if there are amendments, to any amendments to it. The motion helps to narrow the discussion, so everyone is talking about exactly the same things.

The same authorities also say that although this restriction applies to large groups, it can be somewhat relaxed in small groups such as boards and committees. Because there are fewer people involved in a small group, there is less likely to be confusion as participants approach a topic from different angles. Free-ranging discussion can help a small group to come to grips with different aspects of the overall topic and to work out details informally. But this flexibility still requires the chair to make sure the motion brings together all of the important details so the participants know exactly on what they are voting.

A TIME FOR CLARIFICATION

Recently I was retained to serve as parliamentarian for the annual general meeting (AGM) of a large charitable organization. A couple of weeks before the scheduled date for the AGM, the president, André Leduc, pleaded with me, in obvious distress, to sit in on a meeting of the organization's board of directors. He said that a regulation had been introduced that would severely restrict the organization's activities. The board would have to decide how to present it to the organization's general membership at the national AGM. He expected that some board members would use obscure parliamentary procedures to block action and feared he would not know how to handle these procedures.

I attended the board meeting, having agreed to advise if requested to do so. As André had predicted, the board members' discussion became intense and confusing.

After lengthy discussion, André thought it was time to settle the issue. He said, "We have heard from everyone several times. I think it's time to take a vote. Will those in favor please raise their hands?"

I touched his arm, and whispered, "André, I think not everyone knows what is being voted on. Why don't you ask someone to make a motion that is specific, to make sure everyone is on the same page, and can vote for or against it?"

He whispered back impatiently, "If they don't know what this is about they haven't been listening." And he repeated, "Will those in favor raise their hands?" Then, promptly, "Six in favor and I'm in favor so it's seven. Any opposed?" Looking around quickly, he announced, "Five opposed. So, it passes."

You will see several things that the president did wrong, but the one most relevant to this example was his failure to make clear exactly what was being put to a vote. Not surprisingly, the omission had consequences.

Three days later, André phoned me in even greater distress than before. "I'm here with Sharon Forbush, who is the secretary. We're talking about her draft of the minutes. She has written that the board decided to recommend to the members at the AGM that they write personal letters to newspapers to express their opposition to the bill. But when I took the vote, I meant it to be about whether the board should hold a press conference to do so. Sharon and I have agreed we'll go by whatever you decide. Which do you think it was, Dr. Partridge?"

It didn't take me two seconds to know what I would respond. "Well, André, I heard both suggestions being voiced, and discussed. If the two of you aren't sure what was decided, other members will also be unsure. It could create serious divisiveness if you were to go ahead with either position. Have you considered having a brief board meeting to settle this one point? There's probably still time before the AGM."

I felt very proud of myself – I had resisted the temptation to say, "I told you so."

As the preceding example illustrates, it is essential for everyone involved to understand what is being considered, especially when issues are somewhat complicated and have wide potential impact. When we are engaged in discussion, we often direct our minds to what we are going to say next, so we tend to miss some of what others are saying. Besides, it is human nature to hear what we want to hear.

For both of these reasons, unless a discussion is sharply focused, two different participants are likely to have two different recollections of it. A motion, if thoughtfully worded, brings everyone's mind to the same points.

To facilitate this sharpening of attention, you can say, "It seems that we are coming close to agreement on a number of points. Would someone like to make a motion that..." [*and proceed to state as clearly as possible what is being discussed*].

Completing the motion

When someone responds to your request and makes the motion, you may hope that it will include everything needed to achieve its purpose; *who* is to do *what*, and *when*. Unfortunately, what you are likely to hear instead is, "I so move."

This is probably not a good time to explain to all of the participants that to be complete, most motions should state the three key elements. This little bit of education for the participants can take place at some other time but not now in the middle of a discussion. So, for the moment, you will probably accept this weak substitute for a full motion and say, "It has been moved that..." [*and again repeat the content of the motion*]."

(*For a discussion of whether to record the names of movers and possible seconders, see Chapter 9, which discusses the content of minutes.*)

As chair it is your responsibility to state the motion in a form that is adequate and clear, without distorting the meaning that is intended by the maker of the motion. Often the maker of the motion will have spelled out the substance of the motion, that is, what is to be done, but not who is to do it and when.

So you mildly ask, "Who is it that you would like to take responsibility for doing this?"

When this question has been settled you can move to the third key element – the expected time for completion of the tasks in question. You can ask, "When would you like it to be completed [OR a report on it provided to the board]?"

Your question brings to the board's attention that they haven't discussed timing. Yet the way in which you have asked it keeps your question from sounding as if you are criticizing the participants for not having thought about it.

When the participants are generally agreed on all three key elements, you can say something like: "The motion is that [*X*] will be asked to [*do the required tasks*] and report to the board by [*the next meeting?*] Is there further discussion?"

"Wait," you say. "Doesn't each change to the motion have to be done by an amendment that is discussed and voted on?" The answer is "Right – for a *large* group." For a small group, however, just as you can allow discussion before a motion is made, you can also allow informal modification of an incomplete motion, as long as everyone understands what is going on, and they agree.[3] The guideline is to leave enough room for anyone who wishes to raise an objection, while moving the meeting along without wasting time on needless formalities.

OMITTING ESSENTIAL DETAILS IN A MOTION

Several decades ago, when desktop computers were just beginning to become widespread, an acquaintance asked me to provide a legal opinion on a matter

3 See *Robert's Rules of Order Newly Revised*, page 488, referring to a small group: "Informal discussion of a subject is permitted while no motion is pending." *The Standard Code of Parliamentary Procedure* goes further, saying that even in a large meeting it may be useful to discuss a topic informally before shaping a motion.

that was tearing apart the board of a large volunteer organization of which he was president.

He told me that two months earlier the board had unanimously approved the purchase of several computers. The motion approving the purchase had set a maximum price for the purchase, but had not included specifications or said who would make the choice from among competing models.

The executive director, who had held the position for more than twenty years, was on sick leave, so the office manager (OM) was filling in as acting executive director.

To decide which computers to choose, the OM checked with several professionals who had used computers extensively. They all advised either IBM or Apple, and recommended not going to other smaller, perhaps less stable, companies.

The OM reported her findings to the president and with his blessing she ordered IBM models. They were delivered and a company representative trained the OM and several clerks how to use them. All went well for three weeks.

Then the executive director returned to work part-time, saw the computers and exploded. He demanded an immediate meeting of the board. Relying on his long tenure in the association, he demanded that the IBM machines be returned. He explained that he had promised a personal friend, the vice president of the Wang Corporation, that when the company bought computers they would be from Wang. He blustered, "If this doesn't go to Wang, you'll be making a liar of me. Besides, the OM doesn't have the authority to go off like this without my approval."

After a difficult discussion, the board finally agreed and decided to return the IBM machines and purchase their requirements from the Wang Corporation.

And that brings us to the president's request for a legal opinion. When I had heard the whole sad tale, I said to him, "You don't need a legal opinion. Surely you already know that the association can try to break its contract, but that IBM doesn't have to let it off the hook."

I never learned what was resolved with IBM, but I do know that soon the OM resigned to take a better job. And that by coincidence, in a few months the

> Wang Corporation went bankrupt and closed, leaving the new computers without support.
>
> There are several lessons that we might learn from this experience but for the moment we will settle for one - the potential damage that can result when original decisions are made sloppily, without necessary details.

This example may have been an extreme case, but almost every organization has had somewhat similar experiences, in which difficulties have arisen because a decision had been made, but some of the fundamental operational details had not been considered.

A good test is for you, as chair, mentally to review every important decision as it is shaping up, to make sure that it clearly spells out not only the *what*, but also the *who*, and the *when.* And to shape the motion that will lead to a decision so that it is clear, concise, and complete.

You will have brought the meeting to the point where all discussion should be about the same three elements, and not just about one of these elements. If any of the participants think the eventual decision should be to assign the task to someone other than the one(s) named in the motion, they can either propose to amend the motion to substitute a different *who,* or they can ultimately vote against the motion as a whole. Similarly, they can either support, amend, or reject the stated *what* or the *when*. The motion has directed all participants' minds, and their comments, to the same points.

The motion will have focused the discussion so it will be much shorter than it would have been if there had been no motion. Soon you will probably sense that participants have independently made up their minds, either for or against the motion. Then you ask in neutral terms for hands to be raised by those in favor and then, in turn, by those against. And you state whether the motion has or has not been adopted.

It is best for you to state the number of votes cast for and those cast against, and for these numbers to appear in the minutes.

(As explained elsewhere, you do not ask for nor pay any attention to abstentions, which are equivalent to not voting at all.)

Supplying some missing concepts

As chair, since your mind doesn't have to be occupied with what you are going to say in the discussion, you are more free than other participants to notice the fact that some crucial details are missing, and to help lead the other participants to fill those gaps.

If you think they are missing a key point, after most of the others have spoken at least once on the topic it will probably be safe for you to dip a toe into the discussion stream. You will do this only if you feel it is necessary for the group to consider an important point that has occurred to you but that the other participants have overlooked.

Keeping in mind that you do not want to plunge fully into the discussion, you can now present your new concept in a low-key manner. You might say something like, "I wonder if we should consider...."

By using such a soft introduction to your contribution, you help to offset the additional weight that will be given to it just because you are the chair. You are making clear that your suggestion is exploratory and that it is the group that will decide. It also allows you to stop after your contribution, and step back waiting to see if the other participants find merit in what you have said.

Wording your comment as a suggestion that might be considered also avoids any implication that you meant to criticize the participants, as might have been interpreted if you had said, "No one has mentioned...."

If participants pick up and discuss the point you are making, you will feel gratified that you were able to fill a gap in the thinking of the group. If your comment falls flat, however, you cheerfully continue with your position as neutral chair. Unless you feel that not taking up your idea would be disastrous and lead to a very bad decision, you trust the participants to find their way to it, or to find another solution that is better.

Wrapping up the discussion

For most topics, there will come a point at which discussion is beginning to lag. Little new is being said and participants seem less eager to comment. This is a good time to check whether there has been enough discussion on this topic.

"Aren't you glad we had this meeting to resolve our conflict?"

If the discussion has been productive, participants have dropped consideration of several of the points that had been made and that you have reflected in your brief notes (but will omit when you summarize). The participants are now mostly talking about the same things. Hurrah, they are beginning to reach agreement.

You say something like: "I'm hearing you saying...." Then you pick up the major surviving points, giving roughly the same time and emphasis to each, whether you agree with them or not.

Without pausing you go on to say in a neutral tone, "Is there anything *new* we should be adding to the discussion?" A slight emphasis on the word "new" makes the point. If you have judged it correctly, discussion on this topic will taper off and quickly wrap up.

When it does, you can proceed to a vote or to acknowledge approval by unanimous consent.

Sometimes it may not be this easy. You may find that time is running out for the topic and discussion is still unfocused without any indication that the participants are nearing agreement. If you feel that the indecision reflects a concern that there will be unforeseen consequences of a decision, you can suggest a modification that may overcome this reluctance to make a firm commitment.

Relieving anxiety by introducing a sunset clause

It is reasonable for some participants to feel anxiety about possible backlash and side effects that they haven't foreseen, especially if the topic is complicated or controversial. If this becomes a barrier to decision, it has to be dealt with.

One possibility is to suggest that a solution be tried for only a stated period. The approval can have built into it the provision that unless it is formally renewed by another board action, it will expire at the end of the trial period – a month, a year, or whatever is appropriate for the particular topic. Introducing this kind of sunset clause can often ease the way to acceptance of a proposal that otherwise wouldn't have stood a chance of being approved, or if it was approved, it would have been only with reservations.

Voting by the chair

As a member of the group the chair is entitled to a vote but it is wise to use discretion on whether to exercise this right in a particular circumstance. In a large group the chair should vote only in a secret ballot, or if the chair's vote would change the outcome – that is to make or prevent a majority or a required two-thirds vote. This restriction, of course, is to preserve the chair's cloak of neutrality.

In a small group, however, with care and when there is express reason to do so the chair may vote, and may even initiate a motion and enter discussion. Still, when it appears that a decision has already been modified sufficiently that all of the other members will be voting for it anyway, it is better for the chair not to be seen to be voting. This helps to preserve the chair's neutrality and avoids the appearance of possible bias.

Breaking a tie

Some organizations go to great lengths to provide a method for breaking a tie. Some even go so far as to give the chair a second or "casting" vote. Such a provision is highly undemocratic since it would give to one individual the right to make the decision when all of the other members are equally divided.

And it is completely unnecessary.

To take an example, let's suppose that the final vote on a motion is 6 for to 6 against – that is, a tie. The motion has failed to receive the required majority so it fails. There is no hang-up; the decision has been made. The motion has been defeated with no further action needed.

So it is clear that the only special procedures needed in regard to a tie is in an election when equal numbers of votes are cast for two or more nominees for the same position. Suggestions to resolve such a situation are explained in Chapter 8.

Announcing the result of the vote

Whenever a vote is taken it is your responsibility as chair to state what the outcome is, and for the minutes to record how you describe it. There are four possibilities, set out in the following table.

Announcing Voting Results

MOTION OR PROPOSAL	VOTE REQUIRED	THE CHAIR SAYS--
MOST MOTIONS AND PROPOSALS	Majority (more than half) of those voting on the issue	"The motion [or *proposal*] is adopted." OR "The motion is lost for lack of a majority"
ANY THAT REVERSE SOME-THING ALREADY APPROVED, AND ANY THAT RESTRICT A BASIC RIGHT OF THE MEMBERS	Two-thirds of those voting on the measure.	"The motion [or *proposal*] is adopted by the required two-thirds vote." OR "The motion [*or proposal*] is lost for failing to receive the required two-thirds vote."
AMENDMENT OF A BYLAW AND A FEW OTHER SIMILAR SPECIAL CASES REQUIRED BY THE LAW OF THE JURISDICTION.	Two-thirds (or three-quarters, in a few jurisdictions).	"The motion [or *proposal*] is adopted by the required two-thirds [OR *three-quarters*] vote. OR "The motion [*or proposal*] is lost for failing to receive the required two-thirds [*three-quarters*] vote.
ANY MOTION OR PROPOSAL	If no votes are cast against.	"The motion [or *proposal*] is approved unanimously." OR "The motion [or *proposal*] is approved without objection."

Most matters that come before the meeting can be approved by a majority vote, that is one in which there are more votes cast in favor of a particular measure than are cast against it.[4]

Some special actions require more than a majority to be adopted. Examples are actions that rescind or reverse something that was previously adopted, and actions that take away or that reduce basic members' rights in some important way. Examples of restrictions on members' rights are motions that limit or stop discussion or that close nominations. For these special actions, the organization's bylaws, or the parliamentary authority, will usually require a two-thirds vote for approval.

(The simple way to avoid having to go through an arithmetic calculation of two-thirds of the total, is to remember that the number needed is simply twice as many votes cast in favor as are cast against.)

The governing statute or the association's bylaws may require more than a majority for some special actions such as amending a bylaw. In some jurisdictions this requirement is also for a two-thirds vote, in a few other jurisdictions, three-quarters (which means three times as many votes cast for as against).

Whatever the number voting in favor, as long as there is no vote cast against, the measure passes unanimously. The chair should announce that the vote was unanimous, and the minutes must report the result as the chair has announced it.

Unfortunately, some members may object if they purposely didn't vote at all and mistakenly thought that failing to vote would keep the vote from being unanimous. If you think this might happen, to avoid having to deal with a complaint, instead of saying, "The motion is adopted

4 It is sometimes mistakenly said that a majority is "50% plus 1". This is incorrect. To illustrate, if 21 votes are cast, half is 10½ and a true majority (i.e. "more than half") is met by 11 votes. But "50% plus 1" would be 10½ plus 1 or 11½, which would require 12 votes rather than the true majority of 11. The same difference would apply any time there is an odd number of total votes cast. In a close vote, mistakenly having described the requirement as "50% + 1"could make a difference, and lead to controversy.

unanimously," you can substitute, "The motion is adopted *without objection*." Even someone who mistakenly thinks that unanimous means that everyone voted actively in favor, can hardly take offense because they would have to agree that there was no objection voiced.

Special laws sometime require some elected public officials to vote on every issue. Otherwise, no one is required to vote at any time. So, in most cases anyone is entitled to decide not to vote on a particular issue, leaving the outcome to those who do vote.

An abstention is, effectively, a non-vote. It doesn't change the outcome of the vote, nor does it keep a vote from being unanimous. So it would be meaningless, a waste of time, and misleading, if, as is sometimes done, the chair were to call for or to take note of any abstentions.

Closing the meeting

After the participants have made their decisions on all of the major topics, there remain only three more steps to be taken in the meeting.

If there have been no unexpected new topics introduced during the meeting there will be no use directly for the agenda line for Items Received Too Late for the Agenda. The eight minutes allocated for this item has, therefore, been available to provide some flexibility, allowing the major topics to run a bit over the times allocated to them, without causing the meeting to run past its scheduled ending.

Next, you either refer to the scheduled time, day, and date (and place?) of the next meeting or if they are not already fixed, you work with the participants to set the details. If it is necessary to agree on new arrangements, this is easier while the participants are all together than to do so later.

Then you make an obvious point of looking at the time and you say, "It is now 8:29, thank you for your participation. The meeting is adjourned." By formally adjourning the meeting you are drawing a line between what has happened during the meeting, and what may occur afterwards, saving possible later controversy.

You immediately stand up, gather your papers and step back from the table. Removing yourself from the table will tend to discourage those who may be inclined to rehash some of the business of the meeting or to initiate new business that should have been covered during the meeting or that belongs in the next meeting.

If there is a social time planned for after the meeting you participate fully, but avoid to the best of your ability any discussion of business that took place or should have taken place at the meeting. If someone tries to bring up business at the post-meeting social gathering, it's your right, as it is the right of every participant, to say, "Let's hold that until the next meeting. It isn't fair to discuss it now [after some people have gone home] OR [when no-one is prepared to consider it] OR [when we are all tired after a busy meeting]."

After having joined whatever social gathering is arranged, you can go home with a light heart and a well-earned feeling of satisfaction for having planned and facilitated a productive meeting.

We have now covered most of the situations that are likely to occur in every meeting. In the next chapter we will look at the situations that arise in only the occasional meeting but that you will surely encounter from time to time, so are amongst those events for which you need to be prepared.

Chapter 8

Managing Specific Challenges

We all hope for and direct much of our preparation to a meeting that will proceed according to a plan, the shape (although not the subject matter) of which is much the same from month to month. This expectation is appropriate because most regular meetings do follow similar patterns.

Some meetings, however, include situations that are much different from the rest. Some can be planned-for well in advance because you know they will be coming up. Others will be complete surprises, but if you have given thought to the possibility that they might surface you can be prepared even for them so you don't have to improvise on the spot.

Planning for the Annual General Meeting

The annual general meeting is one of the different types of meetings that you will know of in advance, and can plan thoroughly for. The business that it must cover will be specified in the relevant legislation and the organization's bylaws. This relieves you of the need to choose the topics to be covered. It will still be your responsibility to decide to a large extent the order of topics, and how they will be handled.

"I need a list of specific unknown problems that we'll encounter."

One topic that will almost invariably be included is election to the board and to fill other specified positions. Usually a nominating committee has been charged with proposing one or more nominees for each position that will become vacant. The committee recruits possible nominees. At the AGM a representative of the nominating committee presents these names and probably writes them on a white board or a flip chart, so everyone can see them. Having done this, the nominating committee's responsibilities have been fulfilled.

In a number of organizations, a practice has grown up and effectively become an accepted tradition that the person chairing the nominating committee effectively takes over the meeting, presiding over it in place of the meeting chair.

This practice has little logic to support it, and it often makes the meeting unwieldy and confusing.

The Chair of the Nominating Committee has been chosen for personal qualities and experience that have little to do with chairing a meeting. This individual is unlikely to have given as much thought as you have to the techniques of chairing. So the meeting is likely to run more smoothly if you chair it than if someone else does.

Technically, also, the organization's bylaws probably require the chair of the meeting to conduct all meetings when present. Ignoring this requirement, even for a portion of the meeting, could call into question the validity of any nomination or election. So despite any past practice to the contrary, you do not relinquish the task of presiding. Instead, you continue to serve as chair.

You may encounter another situation about which there is often some confusion. While you are chair you may be one of the persons nominated for re-election to another term as chair or to some other position. This still does not give any reason for you to leave the chair during the nominations and elections. Throughout this book the point has been made that the actions involved in chairing the meeting are neutral and as removed as possible from the personal. The procedures for nominations and elections are designed so the acts of chairing are totally transparent, and the meeting chair will act in exactly the same ways regardless of who is nominated.

So, during nominations and elections the chair continues with the same tasks and responsibilities as in any other parts of meetings.

Continuing with nominations

The committee's nominations are only the first step toward election. As chair you are required to invite the members present to make further nominations for each position. Every voting member has the right to nominate one or more additional persons for each position to be filled. As in all nominations, they do not require a second, because by accepting the nomination the person being nominated constitutes a second person who wishes the matter to come before the group.

When you sense that there will be no further nominations for a position, you may ask for a motion and second to close nominations. Since such a motion limits a basic member right – that is, the right to make nominations – its adoption requires a two-thirds vote.

Alternatively, you may feel that everyone would be comfortable if you were to declare approval by unanimous consent for closing nominations for a position.

Election by acclamation?

If there is only one nominee for a position, it is often the practice for the chair to declare that person elected by acclamation. There may be two problems with this practice.

The first possible problem may arise from a strict but accurate interpretation of the organization's bylaws. Some bylaws, in protecting members' privacy, require that elections be conducted by secret ballot. If there is no exception included for the situation in which there is only one nominee, to avoid possible later attack there will have to be some form of election by ballot.

The second possible problem may be less obvious. As is pointed out in *Robert's Rules of Order,* declaring a single nominee elected by acclamation, deprives the members of a right – the right to cast write-in votes. This right, although seldom exercised, allows the voting members to vote for, and if there are enough votes, to elect an individual who has not been nominated. Acclamation, of course, eliminates any chance for write-in votes.

As long as there is no serious controversy within the organization, no one is likely to raise either of these two concerns. On the other hand, in times of serious disruption they are areas of possible vulnerability that could be used to embarrass the chair and the organization.

To avoid this possibility, the bylaws could be amended. Such an amendment would probably expressly allow those present at an election to approve by a two-thirds vote a motion that instructs the chair to declare a sole nominee elected by acclamation.

Proceeding to an election

If there are two or more nominees for a position, there will be a vote. Before the AGM, you will have appointed at least two tellers who are generally seen by the members as being neutral. They will collect and count ballots and report the counts to you. You, not the tellers, will announce the results to the members.

This announcement should include (and the minutes record) not just who received the most votes, but the actual count of valid ballots cast for each nominee.

The organization's bylaws may provide that whoever receives a plurality – that is, the largest number of votes for a position– is elected. If the bylaws do not explicitly state this, however, if there are more than two nominees for a position, balloting has to be repeated until one candidate receives a majority of the votes.

Sometimes two final candidates for a position receive the same number of votes. This situation is unlike a tie in the vote for a motion, which is resolved automatically by the motion having failed to receive a majority of the votes cast on it. In an election there has to be an agreed-upon method to resolve a possible tie.

It would be highly undemocratic if the power to choose were given to one individual or group, such as by giving the chair or some other person a second vote to decide which nominee will be elected. So the rules announced in advance for the election should include a provision that in case of a tie, the tellers will supervise the two candidates as they draw lots to determine the outcome.

The annual general meeting will include other departures from the pattern of a regularly scheduled monthly meeting. Unlike a regular meeting the AGM agenda will usually include the names of several reports (distributed in advance as for any meeting). This does not mean that the reports will be discussed, unless there are specific questions posed by the members about their contents. The purpose of listing those that have been distributed is to make them part of the organization's permanent record for historical purposes.

Handling committee proposals

At times throughout the year, a committee or task force may plan to propose a project that will take large amounts of the organization's time and energy. Such a project might be anything from an extensive public relations or fund-raising campaign to a major restructuring of the parent organization. A proposal this extensive might require so much discussion that it may be desirable for the board to hold a special meeting rather than trying to squeeze it into a regular meeting.

You will know in advance when a committee or task force is going to propose such an extensive program. What you may not know is how the committee or task force leader is expecting to do so.

In similar situations in the past, such a leader may have been allowed to effectively conduct the meeting. However, as pointed out in regard to an election at an AGM, the meeting's progress and results will be better if you continue to chair the meeting. This not only keeps the meeting moving more smoothly, but it also makes it possible for the committee spokesperson to be fully engaged in presenting the recommendations, rather than having also to cope with meeting procedure.

All that is needed to protect against a takeover of the chair's responsibilities is to treat the proposal in the same way as you do any other item of business.

For example, for other business you make sure that relevant documents are distributed to the participants well before the meeting. A major committee proposal should be handled in the same way. The project's purpose, perhaps its history, and what the committee wishes the board to do about it are all spelled out in a written proposal, preferably in point form.

To make sure the proposal is specific enough for the board to consider it meaningfully, it should conclude with the wording of a motion that the committee wishes the board to adopt. As chair, you can have worked with the committee to word the motion effectively so that it includes what is to be done, by whom, and in what time frame.

At the meeting you point out to the members that they have had the material to study for several days. Before discussion begins you invite questions for clarification of any factual or obscure points, asking the committee spokesperson to respond.

Then you invite discussion of the substance of the recommendation. It will probably be most effective if the person who led the committee takes an active part. You can manage this by saying to the participants something like, "Is there any objection to inviting the committee spokesperson to participate in our discussion?" This approach has placed the choice within the hands of the participants. It has also made clear that other members of the committee are not being invited to take part in the discussion, and that they are to allow their representative speak for them. This avoids the chaos that might result if everyone were allowed to jump into the discussion.

Taking a straw vote?

Another situation for which you need to be prepared will arise from time to time. This is when participants appear to be in general agreement with the proposal that is before them, but are still expressing reservations and concerns. You, as meeting chair, have to sense whether what you are seeing is a movement toward real consensus. You have to distinguish between this and what seems on the surface like agreement but instead may be a misleading group dynamic. A few participants may be dominating the group by speaking most often and longest, while others are sitting back, silenced by an unspoken fear that they are the only ones who may disagree.

In such a situation, to test the extent of agreement some chairs resort to what is called a straw vote. This is a vote in which participants are asked to show their current positions by voting for or against the proposal that is being discussed, but with the understanding that this vote doesn't count. It is only to gauge the feelings of the group at the particular moment. Discussion of the topic is expected to resume after the straw vote has taken place, but with everyone knowing how much or how little the proposal has the support of the group.

There are many reports of socio/psychological research that should warn us against straw votes. This research typically consists of telling the research subjects a key "fact" about a topic. This "fact" is completely false, but the subjects are led to believe it is true. Naturally, they form opinions based on the misinformation they have been given.

A week or so later the researchers reveal to the research subjects that the key "fact" was a falsehood, so their opinions are incorrect.

The result? Once having mentally committed themselves to a particular position, the research subjects are unlikely to change that position. In fact, the more information they are given that shows they were originally misled, the more firmly most of them cling to the false belief they had been tricked into forming.

What does this research have to do with a straw vote? Just this: In a straw vote the participants have to commit themselves to either a Yes or a No. As the psychologists tell us, taking a definite position makes it more difficult later for the participants to listen to, and be open to, other positions.

The straw vote freezes opinions, causing the participants to become more fixed in an opinion, which they will mentally – and probably orally – defend, no matter what they hear from others. The straw vote has had the effect of preventing participants from keeping open minds and listening to others' opinions. This, of course, is the exact opposite of the atmosphere that makes for free and open discussion – the atmosphere that you, as a chair, have been working so hard to foster.

So how can you evaluate the sense of the group without taking a straw vote? The answer is to take its measure through use of a "Gradient of Support."

Using the Gradient of Support

The method has to be explained carefully to all the participants. Once they understand and have become accustomed to it, the method can be used to determine whether a discussion is sufficiently advanced to go on to a final decision. It can also be used to help open up discussion when participants seem to be disregarding opposing views or when some seem to be holding back from expressing their opinions.

How does it work?

The term "gradient" refers to a slope that runs from a high position to one that is lower, or from low to high. It may be continuous or it may be in a series of steps. The usual Gradient of Support method has five descending steps.

Using the method, the chair states in clear and concise terms, the main position that is being advocated. Each participant is asked to choose a number from 1 to 5 to indicate that person's level of support for it, with 5 being the greatest.

IF THE PARTICIPANT CHOOSES	IT MEANS
5	I definitely support this proposal and (*if relevant*) I will work to implement it.
4	I agree generally with this proposal, but have some reservations about it.
3	I would be satisfied if this proposal passes, and equally satisfied if it fails.

2	I believe this is not a good proposal, but I'm not sure what would improve it.
1	I believe this proposal is not good; I will offer a substitute that I believe would be better.

This method has several advantages:

- Unlike a straw vote, it does not require the participants to commit themselves prematurely to a firm pro or con position;
- It invites those who choose "4" or "2" to explain their reservations; and
- It absolutely requires those who choose "1" to propose an alternative.

The method makes clear that in most circumstances it is not enough just to oppose something. Responsible opposition includes an obligation to have in mind something that could be better. Especially the obligation for a "1" to propose an alternative may open new ideas that have not been raised before.

Occasionally, a member who registers a 1 believes the better alternative is nothing more than defeating the proposal under consideration. This response, however, would only be justified if the participant believes that nothing could be found that would be better than the existing situation. In other words, that *any* change would be for the worse.

This gradient method emphasizes that instead of choosing sides the group is expecting to continue to work collaboratively to find a solution that is acceptable to all of the participants. They will continue to look for ways to meet existing reservations and to consider fresh alternatives submitted by anyone who registers as a 1.

The method can also help to bring out any remaining opposition instead of leaving it underground where it can fester and later break out into conflict and the creation of opposing factions.

After further discussion of the proposal, modified if possible to reflect the expressed reservations or opposition, you may decide again to use the Gradient of Support method. But it's more likely that you will judge that it won't be necessary to hold another round, and that its first use will have brought enough original thinking into the discussion that you feel the group is ready for a real final vote.

When they vote, of course, participants do have to choose between approval and disapproval of whatever form the proposal has reached. But the decision has to be made and it is understood that the vote brings discussion to an end.

If in the final vote there are still those who oppose the modified proposal, they will be disappointed but they won't feel the group has ridden rough-shod over their concerns. They will know that through the gradient method they have been heard, and their positions have possible been used to modify the original proposal.

Limitations on use of the Gradient of Support

Some organizations use the gradient method, not only for gauging support but also instead of a final yes/no vote. Since 5s and 4s would be taken as being in favor and 2s and 1s as being opposed, little new information would be gained to warrant the extra time needed for the method over a simple vote.

Using the Gradient of Support to replace a simple yes/no vote would also run the risk that participants who are momentarily distracted, might think that a call for a gradient response was being used again to measure support. They could miss the fact that this time it is being used as a final vote. So, it might be best to use the gradient method only for gauging support, and to ask for a normal vote for a final decision.

Some other organizations combine the Gradient of Support method with a commitment that no decision will ever be made unless and until everyone present registers as a 3, a 4, or a 5 – in other words until everyone is satisfied with whatever form the proposal has become.

The requirement for 100% agreement, while perhaps sounding democratic, is actually undemocratic. It gives to any one individual the power to block the group from reaching any decision until it is so watered down that it may be meaningless.

So, there are these limits to its application, but within these limits the Gradient of Support method can be a valuable tool for any meeting.

Providing for minority reports

As discussed in Chapter 1, triangulation can be extremely damaging to any group. A participant whose opinions on an important matter have been rejected by a majority vote may be extremely disappointed. It is natural, then, to want to talk with friends about this disappointment and to explain why the member thinks the group decision was wrong. Sniping at a decision that was made by the board leads to the development of factions and destructive controversy.

The danger is especially pronounced if the topic is complicated, because the outsiders have heard only one side of the issue and have not heard the full discussion that led to most of the participants having supported what became the board decision.

Because of such a possibility some boards adopt a policy under which each participant promises, as a condition of board membership, to support whatever decision is made by the board and not in any way to speak against it outside of the meeting.

This rule is all right for a small, insignificant decision. In many circumstances, it is also best for an important decision. There is one exceptional circumstance in which strict adherence to a rule of board solidarity can unintentionally damage the organization.

Let's suppose that the board has addressed a very important question, intending to take a recommendation to the organization's general membership for approval. Eight board members strongly support Solution A, while the other four board members are equally convinced that Solution A would be a disaster and that Solution B would be much better. When the vote is taken it will come out, of course, 8 to 4 in favor of Solution A.

The board now takes it to the general membership at a general meeting. Because of the vote the board's recommendation is for Solution A. Bound by the rule of solidarity the four board members who favored Solution B cannot mention it to the general members. The general members, trusting the board and being offered no alternative, naturally vote to approve Solution A, the only one they have had presented to them.

But suppose that a large majority of the non-board members *would have voted for Solution B* if they had had it presented to them as a possibility. In this possible situation, the organization has been unintentionally misled by having only Solution A presented.

So how can we adapt a rule of board solidarity to keep disaffected board members from engaging in destructive triangulation, without having to keep the general members in the dark about possible alternatives that they might find preferable?

The answer is to provide for minority reports.

Under this plan, which should be used only for important matters, a minority of the participants who have been outvoted at the board level may announce to the board that they wish to file a minority report. Then two documents are prepared. One sets out and explains the proposal that has been approved by the majority of the board; the other parallel document does so for the position of the minority of board members, who were outvoted at the board meeting.

The board presents both reports to the general membership at the same time. The general members learn about both alternatives, and can choose between them for the benefit of the organization.

The minority report plan avoids triangulation because it is aboveboard; all the board members know it is going to be presented and what it will say. All the general members get the same information at the same time. There is no secrecy and there are no surprises.

The openness shown by a minority report illustrates that the board members are comfortable with differences of opinion, and just want what is best for the organization, even though different board members may disagree as to what the best course might be.

Amending a bylaw

Another question that arises occasionally is how to change the rules under which the organization functions.

An organization is incorporated under an appropriate statute and must comply with the provisions of that law. The organization must have bylaws, and it also may have a constitution or charter. The bylaws, which must not conflict with the governing statute, set out many of the inner workings of the organization.

Sometimes because circumstances have changed since the bylaws were approved it becomes desirable to amend one or more of them. Such an amendment might increase or decrease the number of directors, or change the quorum needed for a general meeting, or make a modification in some other internal operating procedure.

The governing statute of the jurisdiction will specify the minimum steps that must be taken to amend bylaws. The organization's bylaws may add further steps, which must also be followed. Usually the requirements will include having given members sufficient notice of the intention to propose the amendment, the exact wording or a full description of what is being proposed, and eventual approval by a two-thirds (in some jurisdictions, three-quarters) vote of the members.

After the members have been notified of what is being proposed, at the general meeting of members at which the bylaw amendment is being proposed, this wording can be amended by a majority vote. If the modification is significant, this makes it a new proposal. This new proposal has not gone through the required steps to prepare for it to be voted on at this meeting. A new notice must be given to members and a subsequent meeting held for the members to consider and vote on the amended proposal.

Since the bylaw is much like legislation, its wording must be carefully considered and might require professional legal advice.

Resolving an appeal

You may sometimes encounter another semi-legal procedure. Throughout the meeting, as chair you will make many rulings. They may range from whether a motion has passed or failed, to a ruling that something or someone is out of order. Any of these rulings, whether worded formally or informally, is subject to appeal. Although such appeals are more common in a large meeting, they can also arise in a meeting of a board.

Any member may appeal a ruling that has been made by the chair as long as the appeal is made promptly after the ruling. The appeal requires a second. In most cases the person who is presiding is entitled to speak first to explain the ruling, and also last just before the vote on it.

For the vote the chair says, "The question is whether the ruling was correct that....Will those who believe the ruling was correct please raise their hands." Then "Will those who believe the ruling was incorrect please raise their hands."

A majority in the negative overturns the ruling. Otherwise the ruling is sustained.

Just as was explained in the sections about nominations and elections, and contrary to the practice followed by some organizations during an appeal, the person presiding in the meeting should not turn the responsibility over to someone else. The appeal is not about the *person* who is presiding at the meeting; it is only about a disembodied *impersonal ruling.*

Recognizing a conflict of interest

One of the more sensitive matters that you will probably face is when a participant has a conflict of interest concerning a topic that is to be discussed. A conflict of interest itself need not be a cause for discomfort or embarrassment. In today's busy world when people have many different inter-personal relationships, it should come as no surprise for a conflict of interest to arise.

Unfortunately, however, the individual involved will often not have recognized that a particular relationship results in a conflict of interest and may take it as a personal affront when it is pointed out. To help forestall such a reaction you will probably have led a discussion about conflicts of interest when you were helping the group to develop its Code of Conduct (for which see Chapter 1 and appendix A). Even with this advance preparation, however, participants will often fail to recognize their own conflicts of interest.

To protect the organization, therefore, it is essential for the chair to be constantly aware of the possibility of conflicts of interest arising, and to make sure they are properly handled.

When does a conflict of interest arise and what has to be done about it?

The term itself is self-explanatory when the meaning of the words is thought about. A conflict of interest exists when an individual has two different *interests* in a topic that *conflict* with each other. The conflict exists because when fulfilling one interest, the individual must work against the other interest.

Almost everyone recognizes that there is a conflict of interest when a board member has a direct financial interest in a project or a company with which the board is dealing.

It may not be as obvious to some that there is a similar conflict of interest if the board is considering taking some action or stating a position that could *indirectly* relate to a member's interests. Such an indirect, but still real, conflict of interest exists for a municipal board member who is a developer when the board is considering a zoning change, even if it doesn't apply to properties the developer presently owns or has an interest in. Any land developer is inevitably affected by any zoning change or similar regulation because of the precedents it may set.. Nevertheless, many people would deny having a conflict of interest in such a relationship. So it may become a delicate judgment call to decide what to do in such a situation.

Let's take another example that might slip under the radar of many groups. Suppose that as a public-spirited citizen, Gerry is an unpaid member of the boards of two separate volunteer charitable organizations – Advocates for the Homeless (AH), and Fitness for Youth (FFY). As an AH board member, Gerry is committed to doing his very best for AH. As an FFY board member he has an identical obligation to do his very best for FFY.

Let's suppose further that both organizations apply each year to the local United Way for an operating grant. The United Way always receives more requests than it can cover, so whatever amount is approved for one charity will reduce the amount that might be available for other charities. This means that any funds granted to AH will reduce the amount potentially available for FFY and vice versa.

Gerry has a conflict of interest, and cannot take part in any discussion or decisions in either organization relating to operating grants, to United Way, or even to such matters as publicity campaigns that might influence United Way's view of one or the other of these two organizations. Many people would not recognize this situation as a conflict of interest, but it exists nonetheless. It is just as conflicted as any situation in which Gerry might have a personal financial interest.

The interest *may* or *may not* involve some benefit directly to the individual; it is the conflicting interest that matters.

Even more difficult for the chair to explain and require appropriate counter-action is a conflict of interest that involves a personal or emotional relationship that seems completely free from any financial implications.

HOW NOT TO HANDLE A CONFLICT OF INTEREST?

A community organization was planning to appoint a part-time volunteer youth coordinator. The president, Leslie, called a special meeting of the board to discuss the board's earlier interviews with the applicants, which Leslie had not attended.

Leslie chaired the meeting. She opened it by saying, "My daughter, Toni, is one of the three final applicants for the position. Toni has been away from home, supporting herself since she finished college three years ago, so please don't let her connection with me influence your decision." She then took no part in the discussion.

When it came time for the decision, she said, "So there won't be a conflict of interest, I will leave the room while you make the selection. In my absence, will one of you please chair the meeting, and let me know when you have decided which applicant to appoint?"

Not surprisingly, the choice was Leslie's daughter, Toni.

In the example, Leslie tried to disassociate her interests from those of her daughter. No matter how much she protested, however, she would surely have an *interest* in her daughter's hope to be chosen for the position. Toni wanted the appointment, and Leslie would like her daughter to get what she wanted. And the fact that there was no pay associated with the position does not lessen the conflict.

Even though Leslie remained silent, her presence in the room during the discussion might have had an influence (positive or negative) on the board's decision about her daughter.

Other similar types of conflict of interest lurk for the unwary. Because they may not be recognized, it is situations such as these examples that most frequently create problems for boards and their parent organizations, and for the individuals involved.

You may find that a participant doesn't recognize (or admit) being in a conflict of interest. This does not relieve you of your responsibilities in regard to it. Whenever you know the relevant facts, as chair you have no choice but to identify it and to require that it be handled properly.

Any other course leaves you and the group, as well as the individual involved, open to severe criticism. A careless approach can also call into question the validity of any decisions made, and may even end in highly embarrassing legal action.

Handling a conflict of interest

How does a conflict of interest have to be handled? The answer is a legal as well as an ethical requirement. The person who is in conflict of interest *must*:

A) describe to the board the circumstances that result in the conflict; and

B) leave the meeting whenever the topic comes up; and

C) avoid discussing or expressing an opinion or taking any part in dealing with the topic, either within the board meeting or outside of it.

As will be mentioned in Chapter 9, these facts must be recorded in the minutes.

Bypassing the self-appointed parliamentarian

Sometimes you may come onto a board that has a member who continually tries to correct everyone on matters of procedure, but whose knowledge seems to have been accumulated only by observation of what has taken place in other meetings. Experience has shown that such a person's claims are wrong as often as they are right, but they are stated with such assurance that other people tend to accept them at face value.

A simple but common example is for the self-appointed expert to raise a fuss if a motion is being discussed, but the chair has not asked for a second. What the expert doesn't realize is that a second has no purpose except to show that someone in addition to the mover of a motion wants the subject to be brought up for discussion.

When a topic is already being discussed, it shows that other participants are interested in dealing with it, so a second at this stage has no purpose. In a group as small as a board or committee, parliamentary authorities agree that seconds are not necessary anyway. They can be a distraction and a waste of time. Yet, all too often, the self-proclaimed parliamentary expert incorrectly insists on demonstrating supposed superior knowledge.

Other obstructive complaints from such a self-appointed parliamentarian may relate to the timing of a motion, how it is framed, and even to claiming that its subject matter makes it out of order.

If inaccurate advice of this sort would actually make the meeting run smoother, it might not be a problem. Instead, the incorrect advice is often designed to advance some particular purpose, is unfair to some participants, and misdirects the meeting. At the very least, it can be an interruption and a distraction.

When similar occasions happen frequently, it may be necessary to protect the group from this kind of aggravation and possible misdirection.

HELPING TO EDUCATE A SELF-PROCLAIMED PARLIAMENTARY EXPERT

A friend in a nearby city asked me to attend and advise at a few meetings of the seventeen-member board of a seventy-year-old charitable organization. My friend was having difficulty keeping the president from resigning out of frustration, just as the previous president had done.

Every time the president made a ruling, Ronald, a long-time and particularly assertive member, would say the ruling was contrary to *Robert's Rules of Order*. The self-appointed parliamentarian would then lecture the group, claiming broad knowledge of meeting procedure and implying that everyone else was ignorant of it. My friend and the president, both doubted that this individual knew what he was talking about, but they didn't know what to do about it.

I attended the next board meeting. The president introduced me as a practicing parliamentarian and said that he would rely on me for advice as to details of procedure.

Soon after the meeting began, Ronald interrupted and said, "Dr. Partridge, you are a parliamentarian. Isn't it illegal to include two entirely different subject matters in a single motion?" (Afterward, my friend told me that this had been an issue that Ronald had made much of after the previous monthly meeting.)

I responded, "Well, it's certainly not illegal because it doesn't fall under criminal or civil law. But, yes, it is probably unwise because the members should be able to discuss and vote separately on each of the two subjects. However, if you ever think a motion includes two different ideas, all you have to do is move to divide the question. If it is seconded, a majority vote will divide the motion. There are even some situations in which a single member can require that a motion be divided. If you would like details on this simple procedure you could look up a copy of *Robert's Rules of Order, Newly Revised*. You can read about this simple procedure starting at page 270."

Ronald flushed. He didn't speak again for the rest of the meeting. My friend told me later that Ronald did not attend the next two monthly meetings, and then he resigned. And from then on the board meetings went smoothly and without the previous aggravations.

I was probably more harsh than I should have been but it seemed justifiable at the time.

Rarely, a member becomes so disruptive that drastic action is needed. But it is more likely to occur if the organization has not developed a procedure to deal with interpersonal conflict at its early stages.

Arming yourself for parliamentary maneuvers

If you don't want to take the time to become a real parliamentary expert yourself, there are still three simple defenses against feeling uninformed about parliamentary procedures. First is to familiarize yourself with a summary of the most common procedures that you will encounter. You can do this relatively quickly by digesting the brief summary in Appendix B of this book. Second, you glance through and generally familiarize yourself with the accompanying summary procedural steps that might be useful in a typical meeting. Keeping this list handy during a meeting allows you, if one of these procedures is suggested, to check quickly to see which steps are open to discussion and which are not, as well as to know whether this procedure can be approved by a majority vote or if it needs a two-thirds vote. With these simple preparations, you are covered for most common meeting procedures so you can avoid glitches that might embarrass you or that would give an opening to the self-proclaimed expert.

A third defense should resolve any remaining unanswered situations. During a meeting, if a procedural question arises about which you haven't read or have forgotten what to do about, there's no need to feel embarrassed. There are not many presiding officers who have at their fingertips the contents of all 700-plus pages of *Robert's Rules of Order, Newly Revised*. So you needn't feel you have to pretend that you have done so.

The group cannot override a clear provision of the governing statute or of a bylaw that provides members with a basic meeting right. However, if the issue is how to interpret one or the other in relation to a particular circumstance, you can put it to the group. You do not leave an opportunity for the self-appointed parliamentarian to express an opinion or to propose a ruling. You just confidently say, "I'm not sure how this should be handled. We could...or alternatively we could...." Then you put it to a vote of the group.

You follow whatever the group decides upon, as long as the decision does not unfairly limit the rights of members, absent or present. What the group decides will over-ride *for this group, for this meeting*, whatever parliamentary books may say on the subject. And you won't be saddled with faulty and possibly self-serving advice from the participant who would claim special knowledge but who may or may not know the published answers.

Expelling a member

You may never face the need to expel a member of the board or of the organization. But if there is absolutely no other solution to a serious conflict, you should be warned that this situation has many possible pitfalls.

Make sure that you have the complete story. Because you know some people better than others, you will probably have heard one side of the story more completely than the other or than any of the others (and there are usually several stories). The fact that the conflict exists means that the interpersonal relationships are complex.

It is tempting to take the easy route and lay the blame on one of the antagonists. Then, without recognizing your bias, you see the other as a victim. In fact, everyone involved is a victim because no sane person enjoys a conflict.

It does little good to try to uncover what event or contact was the starting point for what grew into a conflict. Instead it is more helpful just to acknowledge that a conflict exists and to use all of your skill and good will to resolve it.

If informal consultation does not heal the rift, the organization may wish to retain a professional mediator.

If mediation has been unsuccessful and the conflict is seriously hurting the organization, as a last resort you may be faced with the need to remove one or more members from the board, committee, or organization. Of course, this cannot be a unilateral decision by the chair or by anyone else. It must be a deliberate decision thoughtfully considered by the board, or by a general meeting of the members, or by whatever procedures are mandated by the legislation and the bylaws.

The organization's bylaws may (and in fact, should) give explicit directions as to how to expel an officer or a member. But regardless of how detailed those directions may be, the board also needs expert legal advice. Many attempts to expel someone eventually end in court. Then the organization may face serious difficulties because of things that were innocently but inadvisably said and done *before* legal advice was sought.

So if the situation comes to this unfortunate and unpleasant stage, *run, don't walk*, to a legal firm that is experienced in these matters, and then insist that everyone follows to the letter any legal advice that is received.

Now you are well prepared for many of the situations that are most likely to arise while you are chair. Each difficult situation may look a bit different, but almost all will fit within some of the patterns that have been described in this and the previous chapter.

The impact on the organization as a whole will depend in part on how the meeting is reported and how its decisions are made available to the organization's members and perhaps to the general public. This is the subject of the next chapter.

Chapter 9

Making The Decisions Effective

All of the preceding chapters in this book have been directed toward making more effective your mentoring, facilitating, and managing of meetings. The primary focus has been on your advance preparation and on increasing your skill in conducting the meeting to improve the group's decisions and decision-making.

Decisions, however, are not an end in themselves. The best possible decisions have value only when the people affected by them have prompt, ready access to them currently and when needed in the future.

Informing individuals of meeting decisions

When you declare the meeting adjourned, your job as chair is not finished. You still are responsible for three crucial tasks. The first of these remaining tasks is to ensure that everyone who will be directly affected by the decisions that have been made are aware of what has been decided and of what actions each individual is expected to be taking.

If you were to follow a strict division of duties among the organization's officers, this communication task would fall to the secretary. In the practical world, however, it probably works better as a collaborative effort between the secretary and the chair. It is not easy to think of everyone who might be affected, so if the two of you discuss it and divide the task between you, you will be more likely not to overlook someone who should be informed.

The other two tasks are connected, with the third building on the second. They both relate to making and keeping a record of the decisions that were made in the meeting. One task records the decisions for current use; the other sorts and preserves them for ready availability in the future.

First, let's look at why we want to keep a record of the meetings.

Keeping the record

Immediately after a meeting, each of the participants will remember it differently. Some participants will remember best those decisions that were the most difficult to arrive at. Others will especially remember some discussions in which they changed their minds. Still others will carry in their minds those decisions that supported or rejected proposals in which they were most interested. No two participants will recall the meeting in the same way.

As time passes and memories fade, these differences will become even greater. Yet, it is important for there to be one, and only one, official record of the meeting. This common viewpoint can only be achieved if there is a written record of the meeting. But, what kind of a written record is most effective and useful?

Selecting the appropriate kind of record

There are at least three different kinds of written record of a meeting. Each serves a different purpose.

One kind of record is a transcript that records everything that has been said. It is the type of record that is kept in a court proceeding because any single syllable might help to prove or disprove an allegation. A transcript's length and its cost would not make it suitable for the types of meetings that this book addresses.

A second kind of written record is often referred to as a meeting's proceedings. It includes expressions of ideas, suggestions, and other summaries or descriptions of what has been said and done. It is less complete than a transcript but is still extremely long and detailed, and because of its nature it's usually rather unfocused. This kind of record is suitable for a convention, a retreat, a workshop, or for any other gathering in which the purpose is to provide information and to invite opinions and reactions but not necessarily to make decisions.

The third kind of meeting record is the one that is appropriate for the type of meeting that this book is primarily about. Called "the minutes" this record is shorter, tighter, and more limited than the other two kinds of record. It serves a different purpose than the other two because the meetings that it reports have a different purpose – deliberation and discussion that lead to decision-making.

Recognizing the purpose of minutes

It is only when we consider something's real purposes that we can design it to be most effective in accomplishing those purposes. This is as true of minutes as of anything else. So let's look a little deeper at their purpose.

I once asked each of eight friends individually what they saw as the purpose of minutes. I knew that each of them had attended many meetings and that some had served as the president or the secretary of one or more boards or organizations. They had all worked extensively with minutes, and some had been responsible for drafting them.

One of the eight was a lawyer. Not surprisingly, he viewed minutes primarily as a source of reliable evidence. He was right but only in a limited sense.

The other seven took a more conventional view. They thought my question was slightly silly since to them the answer was obvious. All seven responded in almost exactly the same words. They all believed that the purpose of minutes was to *describe what happened in a meeting.*

My question was certainly not a scientific survey. Even so, it was striking how similar the answers were to my question from seven different people who all had broad experience with meetings. Their responses may give us some clues as to what many other people think about minutes. Their answers may also explain why so often minutes are written as they are, that is, to try to re-create a meeting.

"Here are the minutes of our last meeting. Some events have been fictionalized for dramatic purposes."

A social psychologist might be interested in what actually happened in a meeting, but unless some interpersonal relationship arose that created a problem, it would be of little interest to the group's members or to members of the parent organization. There must be other purposes for minutes, or we wouldn't bother to keep them.

When we think about it, we realize that it is not the *meeting* that we want to describe in a permanent record. What people on the board and within the organization want and need to know is what decisions were made and how those decisions can be known and applied. In most cases, it doesn't matter *how* a decision was reached; the essence is *what* was decided. Thought of in this light, it becomes clear that the real purpose of minutes is to *record decisions* in ways that make their meanings *available* for future reference.

Another way to look at the purpose of minutes is that they are to *guide future action.* Minutes that are written so they focus on describing what happened in a meeting that has been completed and adjourned would be looking to the past; those that focus on guiding future action are looking to the future. It is these points that we will be looking at in detail throughout the rest of this chapter.

Choosing what to record in the minutes

Even if we wanted to, it would not be practical or informative to try to record everything that was said and done during the meeting.

Some things said during a meeting may have been completely disregarded by the other participants. Should these comments become part of a permanent record? Probably not. Other comments may be incomplete and may not express the participant's final opinions. It would not accurately report the discussion to include these temporary expressions of opinion. Still other comments may have influenced some participants to begin to think along the lines that later become the group's decision. In that case, aren't those comments adequately reflected in the final decision? These and other similar questions about bits of discussion raise the question of how to choose what to include in minutes.

Of most concern, however, is that since it isn't feasible to include everything in minutes, it is necessary to omit some things, while including others. Unless other arrangements are made, the selection has to be somewhat arbitrary, depending on which comments the secretary thinks at the time may be most important. Two different secretaries at the same meeting would make different choices as to what bits of discussion to reflect. As a result, if this is how the selections are made, the result will become, in effect, "the secretary's minutes" rather than "the meeting minutes." Not a good solution, even though it is the one that is reflected in the record of many meetings.

MINUTES THAT ARE ACCURATE BUT MISLEADING

A few years ago, I was a member of the board of the regional chapter of a large national organization. We had learned that the national officers were planning to make a proposal at the upcoming national convention that we believed was unwise.

A member of the board of our chapter made a motion that we send a letter to the national office asking the national board to withdraw the proposal. Early in the discussion of the motion I said, "A single letter won't have much effect. I think *instead* we should use our efforts to urge other chapters to instruct their delegates to vote against the proposal at the convention."

Our secretary had always tried to record in the minutes all relevant discussion. To do this she had to decide which comments were important and which were of only passing interest and therefore not to be included in the minutes. As she had diligently made notes, she apparently picked up the first part of my comment because when the draft minutes were presented for approval at the next meeting one line said, "Bruce said that we should not send a letter."

This, of course, was accurate as far as it went, but it had completely missed what I had considered the most important portion of my suggestion – that we enlist other chapters to join us at the convention in opposing the proposal.

But this wasn't the greater problem. I had done what we hope will sometimes result from free and open discussion – I had changed my mind! (If people didn't change their minds sometimes, why bother to have discussions?) After

I had expressed my preliminary view, another board member had told us that several other local chapters had already written expressing the same views that we held. Consequently, instead of our letter being a lone complaint, it would add weight to the expression of widespread concern. When I heard this, I thought that sending a letter was a good idea.

When the chair eventually took a vote on the motion to send a letter, the result was 7 to 1 in favor. I was one of the seven who voted for the idea that I had originally spoken against.

At the next meeting, when the minutes came up for correction, the only reference to my position on the subject was that I had said we shouldn't send a letter. I didn't think it was worth using meeting time to insist on having the minutes explain my change of mind. As a consequence, the permanent record continues to imply incorrectly that I had been the one board member who had voted against the motion.

In retrospect I recall this incident as a classic example of how a secretary's honest attempt to record details of discussions can be factually accurate as far as they go, but because they are necessarily incomplete can provide a false picture.

Recording some elements of discussion?

Discussion takes up the majority of the time in most meetings. Does this mean that it follows that the majority of the space in minutes should also be devoted to discussion? Not at all. We have to choose what portions, *if any*, of discussion should be included in the minutes. To help with that choice we might look at what typically happens in discussion.

Let's suppose that during the meeting, participant Alice says something about a proposal that is one of the main topics on the agenda. Then participants **B**ritt and Chester add comments, either agreeing or disagreeing with, or completely disregarding whatever she has said. Next Duane makes a motion that is eventually voted on and approved.

What are the important aspects of these exchanges? Of course, it is crucial for the minutes to report the wording of the motion *as it was passed* (after any amendments had been approved).

How about whatever **A**lice, **B**ritt, and **C**hester have said about the topic? If their inputs resulted in shaping the motion, their views are already reflected in it. So why repeat what is already covered?

On the other hand, if what they said didn't shape what the group eventually decided, what difference do their remarks make? Why keep a permanent record of something that added nothing to what was eventually agreed upon?

The result is that whether what they said did or did not influence the decision, their discussion doesn't help to define the decision that was eventually made. Therefore, there is no reason to record it.

Sometimes it might be significant to record whether a matter was decided after detailed deliberation, or with less deep consideration. If this might be relevant, the secretary can preface the wording of a motion by writing something like, "*After extensive discussion*, Sheryl moved that..." or "*After brief discussion*, Samuel moved that...," and so forth. If it is not relevant, any reference to discussion is superfluous and doesn't add anything.

Another factor to consider is how the minutes will be used in the future. When deciding if a particular bit of information should appear in the minutes, another good question to ask is: "Could this information help to guide future action?" If so, it probably should be included in the minutes; if it does not, why clutter the minutes with things that have little or nothing to do with how the organization will function in the future?

Later in this chapter this issue will be explored in greater detail but for the moment let's visualize someone a few years after the meeting wanting to know what has been decided on a particular matter.

If the minutes run to half-a-dozen pages for each monthly meeting, the person will have to dig through a hundred or more pages just to find the few lines that report this one decision. In the process, the person searching might give up, and never find the relevant passage in the accumulated copies of past minutes. In such a case, the minutes have served no purpose whatsoever.

Another possibility is that the person might find one decision about the topic and stop searching. In doing so, he or she might fail to discover that tucked away in the minutes of another meeting a related decision reversed or changed the effect of the first.

Either result would be misleading and would discourage anyone in the future from making the effort to check past minutes. If no one is going to look at them in the future, a reasonable question is: "If they won't be referred to and will just take up shelf space, why bother to keep them?"

Democratically selecting what to include

There is a simple democratic solution to the question of how to decide what to include in minutes and what to omit. This is to agree in advance with the secretary that the minutes will include only such parts of discussion and decision as you, the chair, have expressly indicated.

It might appear that this would be undemocratic as well as awkward. But in practice it is neither. In fact, it works smoothly, without fanfare. And it is completely democratic.

You might ask, "How could it be more democratic for the chair to select what to include rather than for the secretary to make the selections?" The answer is that it is NOT the chair, but the group that has made the selection.

How can this be? We have already gotten away from any thought of trying to report the discussion, so we now have to consider only the decisions. As described in Chapter 7, as the meeting progresses and each topic is ready for decision, the chair states the wording of the motion (or the informal proposal) before putting it to a vote or declaring it approved by unanimous consent. At this point, the chair will nod to, or otherwise make eye contact with, the secretary to give an alert that this is the wording that is to go in the minutes.

When the vote is taken, or the matter is approved by unanimous consent, this wording is exactly what the participants had in their minds and therefore what they approved as a group. If the chair's wording hadn't been fully acceptable to all participants, they would have changed it. So, the participants will have had the last word. Following normal procedures by using these words, what will go in the minutes will be what the *group* has decided (or rejected), and is not what any one individual has chosen. How could anything be more democratic?

Recording other facts

There are a few other bits of information that we will wish to know at some time in the future, and we will also want to identify which meeting the minutes are from. Those that will need to be in the minutes include:

- ✓ The name of the group;
- ✓ The date the meeting was held;
- ✓ Whether it was a regular meeting, or one called for a special purpose;
- ✓ Who chaired the meeting, and who served as secretary;
- ✓ That a quorum was present, and when, if ever, the quorum ceased to be present;
- ✓ The names of those who attended and those who were excused (or for a large group, the number of voting delegates who were present); and
- ✓ If relevant, the names of special guests.

All of these items appear at the top of the first page of the minutes. For an illustration, see the sample minutes below.

When a vote is taken, the minutes record the number of votes cast in favor of a proposal and the number cast against it, as well as whether it passed or failed. If the particular measure requires more than a majority, such as a two-thirds vote, this too is reported in the minutes.

If there were vote(s) cast for a motion or proposal and none cast against it, it doesn't matter that some of those present did not vote at all. By definition, as long as there were no votes cast against it, it has been carried unanimously. The chair will declare the vote unanimous, or without objection as mentioned above. This fact is also recorded in the minutes.

If a latecomer enters after the meeting begins, the minutes must reveal the place in the business of the meeting where this occurred. This makes it possible to know which discussions and which votes this participant was present for. The minutes can say something like: "During the discussion of the following motion, Monty joined the meeting."

A similar entry would be made for any participant who leaves the meeting before its adjournment.

If a participant has declared a conflict of interest, (see Chapter 8) the minutes explain the nature of the conflict of interest and where in the business of the meeting the person involved left and returned to the room, as well as the fact that the person did not take part in discussion or any vote on the issue.

Recording movers and seconders, times and places?

It can be assumed that the person who makes a motion supports it. The person who seconds it, however, may actually oppose it, and may be providing a second only so it can be brought before the group so it can be defeated.

So the chair states and the minutes record the name of the motion's mover but not of its seconder, if there is one.

Some parliamentary authorities suggest and many groups have the habit of reporting the exact time at which a meeting was called to order and also the time at which it was adjourned. The question has to be asked: "Would any of the decisions that were made have any different meanings or effects if the meeting had commenced at 7:03 than if it had been opened as scheduled at 7:00?" Obviously, not, unless there is some special reason that time is crucial.

The same question applies to the time of adjournment, with the same answer.

Unless there is some unusual reason to need to know the exact times, this appears to be nothing but the type of clutter that we are trying to eliminate from minutes. So, unless you believe there is a special implication related to starting and stopping times, why not disregard them?

It might contribute further pointless clutter to record where the meeting was held, unless there is some special reason to record this information. If the group's meetings are always held in the organization's boardroom, why continually record this fact? If, on the other hand, successive meetings have to migrate from location to location, it might help with participants' memories of what occurred at a particular meeting (and might explain a participant's absence) to report where each meeting was held.

For any unusual matters, the test of whether to have it included in the minutes is whether having the information available might be useful at some time in the future. If there is doubt, it would be good to err slightly on the side of inclusion, because if it is not included the information may be lost forever.

Including other possibly useful information

If an archive by category has not yet been created (as described later in this chapter), it may help future searchers of the collected minutes to include in bold-face type a marginal title for each decision. If it is decided to include such identifying titles, it is important for them to be neutral in effect.

One way to make sure of neutrality is to use the same wording for the marginal title as appeared as a line item on the agenda. Otherwise, some personal bias might unintentionally creep in.

It becomes a question of judgment whether reports that have been received should be attached to the minutes. The board members have already received and presumably read them, so in most cases they hold no further information for the participants.

Any reports that include recommendations that were acted upon might be of some use in explaining decisions in the future. Those that are not confidential might be of interest to other members of the wider organization. A collection of reports that relate to the organization's activities might some day be of use to reconstruct a history of the organization. So it may be advisable to keep a copy of each report, filed either chronologically, or by major topic, or by its source. To avoid overwhelming the minutes, if they are kept, it should be in a separate archive.

Approving minutes

The minutes are the formal record of decisions made. It is important for them to be carefully and thoughtfully prepared and handled subsequently. Their approval should not be casually automatic, but must be conscientiously considered to make sure that they are complete and accurate, and that they do not contain unnecessary material that obscures the important portions.

Since the minutes are primarily limited to decisions that have been made and since they reflect what the group itself has decided, there will seldom need to be any corrections. However, participants should always have the opportunity to correct any errors that are in the draft before they approve it.

Some organizations provide for a two- or three-person committee to review and approve minutes, rather than having them placed before the group as a whole. Unfortunately, this committee usually consists of the chair and the secretary, with perhaps one other member. This could lead to the possibility (and in some cases the actuality) that by manipulating the meeting's minutes, insiders could effectively control what appears to have been the decisions that have been made. Even if the power is not abused, the appearance of undemocratic practices can erode trust within the group.

A better procedure is for the secretary to prepare the minutes and the chair to distribute the draft to all of the members of the group well in advance of the next regular meeting (as suggested in Chapter 5). This gives the participants enough time to review the draft at their leisure and to be ready at the next meeting to suggest corrections if any are needed.

Controlling unapproved drafts of minutes

Before a draft of minutes is finally approved, corrections may be made in it. Several copies of the unapproved draft will have been in circulation because they will have been shared with members of the group and perhaps with others while still in draft form. After the minutes are formally approved, participants cannot be relied on or even expected to return to the secretary their draft copies for replacement with final, approved copies. As a consequence, copies of the draft that has not been approved may be around for several years.

If there has been a correction, the earlier drafts will not include it and can therefore be seriously misleading. But if there were no corrections, the original drafts will be identical to the approved copies. How can anyone know, then, if a copy marked "draft" is or is not the same as the copy that has been finally approved?

This is an unofficial, unapproved draft. It may differ from the approved minutes unless the final page includes a notation showing by what group and when it has been approved.

FRIENDS OF THE MUSEUM

REGULAR MEETING OF THE THE BOARD **DRAFT**

Wednesday, October 14, 2xxx

MINUTES

The president, Shannon Finnerty called the meeting to order and noted that a quorum was present. Minutes were kept by secretary, Abe Crandall.

All members were present except Jane Adelle who had advised the president that she would be out of town.

It was AGREED that Greg would request curator Sasha Deutsch to describe the new fossil acquisitions, at the November 5 meeting of members, ACTION

After lengthy discussion, Kyle moved that up to $450.00 be budgeted from the Contingency Fund to transport the Sandhurst Collection from Springfield. Approved by a vote of 5 to 1.

On recommendation of the By Laws Committee, it was:

RESOLVED as a Special Resolution that the ByLaws be amended by adding the following Section:

"5.1.4. Effective immediately the annual dues of all Honorary Members be waived."

After lengthy discussion the Special Resolution received a vote of 5 to 3. Having failed to meet the requirement for a two-thirds affirmative vote, the Special Resolution failed.

The president declared the meeting adjourned.

_/s/___________________________________

Secretary

APPROVED BY: Date: (dd/mm/yyyy) Signed:

☐Board

☐Other

There is an easy way to avoid this confusion. As part of the minutes, the secretary places a header at the top of *each page* that consists of a cautionary note as illustrated.

When the minutes of a meeting have been approved, the secretary makes the proper notation on the last page of the official file copy, showing the approval authority and date of approval, and signs in the appropriate box to verify that it is official.

Participants will need to be reminded that if they keep any copies of the draft minutes, they should fill in the data about the approval when it takes place. But if some forget to do this, there will be no harm done because of the warning note on all pages.

Creating an accessible permanent record

Most organizations keep a Minute Book, which contains, in chronological order, the minutes for meetings of the board. They also keep a similar Minute Book of General Meetings of the members. These are probably necessary to meet legal requirements, and even if it were not, it should be done.

Usually, only members of the board have access to board minutes, while all members of the organization have the right to see minutes of general meetings of members. So, to simplify control of access, it is best to keep the two in two separate books or files.

These Minute Books are not, however, convenient for someone in the future who might want to know what the organization's policy is for a particular matter.

To find such a policy, the searcher would have to read through page after page of minutes, searching for a motion that has established the policy. The result is that most people don't bother to take the time to make such a search. Thus, they don't know of and can't follow any policy that has been approved and is presumed to govern action but has been effectively forgotten.

If decisions related only to immediate issues, it might not matter for them to be forgotten soon after they have been approved and acted upon. But some decisions are intended to set ongoing policy for the future.

Keeping decisions current and available

Minute Books, regardless of whether they are in hardcopy or electronic, will be kept chronologically by the dates on which the meetings were held. To find a particular policy decision someone would have to know the date of the meeting in which the decision was made. Without knowing the date a policy was approved, someone searching for it would have to dig through many pages of minutes to find a particular decision. If the file is being kept electronically, key-word searches might find some relevant decisions, but others might be missed unless the searcher is lucky enough to guess the wording of any decisions that touch on the topic being researched.

The following example (which occurred exactly as described) illustrates how minutes can effectively disappear shortly after they are approved, unless they are specially handled.

LOST(?) POLICY

The finance committee of a community organization was beginning to regularize some of the policies relating to the organization's financial practices. One of these policies was designed to state how the organization would handle future gifts of art works. This was thought necessary because sometimes people offered works of art that were felt not to be in keeping with the organization's décor. Also, sometimes the donor would request a charitable receipt for an amount far greater than the work could be sold for on the open market, which could raise questions with tax authorities.

The finance committee considered the question at two successive meetings. It agreed on and proposed to the board a policy to cover the situation. After some discussion, the board approved the proposed three-step policy, agreeing that it would:

1. Refer any such gift to the aesthetics committee to decide if it was suitable; and
2. If found suitable, retain a qualified appraiser to set its real value; and
3. Issue a charitable receipt for that value.

The approved policy was recorded in the Minute Book. Two and a half years later, much of the membership of both the board and the finance committee had changed. Only two of the original board members remained, and only one of the original finance committee members. The continuing finance committee member became its chair.

A supporter offered to donate a painting. The two carryovers on the board and the one on the finance committee, respectively, had all forgotten the discussions that had taken place three years earlier. At the time, it had been presumed that the policy would govern all similar situations. However, when the identical situation arose later no one thought to dig through the many pages of minutes (which had always reported large amounts of discussion!).

The now-current finance committee members wrestled with the question, taking up considerable meeting time. Finally, the finance committee agreed on a draft policy, which it recommended to the board. The board, after some discussion, approved the proposed policy. This "new" policy, when discussed and finally approved, provided that when offered a gift of an art work, the organization would:

1. Refer the offered gift to the aesthetics committee to decide if it was suitable; and
2. If found suitable, retain a qualified appraiser to set its real value; and
3. Issue a charitable receipt for that value.

Does this sound familiar? Actually, the words that were used were slightly different, but the effect was identical to the "policy" that had been labored over and approved only three years earlier.

Three people had not remembered and the others had not known that the policy already existed, because it was buried in the many pages of minutes from more than thirty monthly meetings. And not knowing that it even existed, no one had thought to look for it. So they had to use considerable meeting time and energy both in the finance committee and in the board to come up with what had already been done once.

This example is not unique. The people involved probably were neither more nor less likely than the average person to have remembered that the same subject had come up and a policy had already been approved for it.

To avoid wasteful duplication of time and effort, there has to be a simple, easily addressed method to find if the topic of interest has been decided in the past, and if so, how it was decided. Fortunately, such a method exists. It is a file of decisions that are sorted by category of subject matter rather than by the dates on which they were approved.

Keeping important decisions readily available

To set up the system the board (or the chair and secretary) decide what categories best fit the organization. Depending on the organization's interests and activities, a possible starting point for some organizations might be something like: Events, Finance, Government Relations, Membership, Publications, and Seminars. An organization that owns a building, or that is a home owners' association (in the U.S.) or strata council (in Canada) might choose categories such as: Building Maintenance, Contingency Fund, Landscaping, Parking, Pet Restrictions, and Security.

When the categories have been selected, a segment of the archive would be opened for each one, whether hard copy or electronic.

After each meeting, while the secretary still has the minutes in a computer file, it is easy to copy and paste each approved motion to a separate, pre-designed, full-sized cover sheet such as the abbreviated sample below.

<table>
<tr><td colspan="2">FRIENDS OF THE MUSEUM
APPROVED MOTIONS</td><td>CATEGORY

☐Policy</td></tr>
<tr><td colspan="3">TEXT OF MOTION AS APPROVED:
______________________</td></tr>
<tr><td>APPROVED (dd/mm/yyyy)
☐Unanimous
☐Vote ____ to ____</td><td colspan="2">BY
☐Board
☐General Meeting
☐Other ___</td></tr>
</table>

Of course, the secretary completes the blanks on each cover sheet, and then files them by category, keeping each category in a separate section.

Some motions will fall under more than one category. For example, a motion dealing with membership dues would fit in both categories of Finance and Membership. For such motions the secretary makes two cover sheets, one for each category. Then someone in the future will have two possible routes to pursue, and will be most likely to find the motion, regardless of whether it's being thought of as a financial matter or as one that relates to membership.

It may take some time and thought to decide what categories to set up for the organization. However, once the system is in place, it takes only a few moments to handle the relatively few motions from each monthly meeting as soon as the minutes have been approved. And it makes it possible for everyone easily to find later what has been decided, so the board's actions are not lost in the mists of time.

Following up after the meeting

Although board members will know of all decisions the board makes, they may not make a note of whatever action is expected of them individually. To protect against this possibility, in drafting the minutes the secretary puts the word "ACTION" after each motion that requires someone to do something. For the board members this will serve as a reminder when the draft minutes are distributed for review. For actions that are expected from non-board members, the caption will alert the chair to make sure the individual is informed of the decision.

You have devoted your efforts to helping the group to make the best decisions of which it is capable, and now to recording those decisions clearly and in ways that make them most useful, both currently and in the future. A quick look at the appendices that follow will give you some additional tools that will make your work easier and more effective. Then you can look forward to mentoring and leading the group to meetings that are productive and pleasant, and of which everyone can be proud.

Appendix A

Practical Codes of Conduct

There are many different types of codes of conduct, each serving a different purpose. A code in a business organization is a tool of management. It sets out how management expects its employees to function, usually with primary focus on customer relations. A code of conduct for a volunteer organization as a whole is likely to cover such subjects as supporting the organization's purposes, following its precepts, and dealing with interpersonal conflict.

A third type of code of conduct is appropriate for the board of an organization, regardless of whether it is volunteer, homeowner, religious, charitable, or some other kind that meets to discuss and to make decisions affecting itself and the parent organization. It covers how the participants will deal with each other, both within and outside of its meetings; how they will handle discussion and decision-making; avoidance of triangulation; and often, the extent to which matters within its meetings will be held confidential.

Unlike the other two types of codes mentioned above, this type can be truly effective only if it is created by the participants themselves and each of them signs on to it in the fullest sense. The choices of subjects to be included and the decisions as to how they are to be worded are less important than the process of arriving at them.

One approach to creating this type of code of conduct is to start with a brainstorming session. It is crucial that all of the participants be present and take an active part in the process. They will suggest topics that they believe should be included. Near the end of the session, they discuss and collectively select from the long list that has been generated, those topics that they collectively feel best fit their group and how they would like it to function.

Then they delegate to one or at most two of their members the task of preparing a first draft that includes the selected topics. Trying to draft by committee is notoriously difficult and almost invariably produces a mediocre, wordy, mushy, failed attempt to please everyone.

In drafting the code, the most effective wording makes direct reference to specific action, rather than to broad principles. For example, a statement such as: "We will give everyone equal opportunities to speak" means much more to the participants than: "Speaking order will be determined equitably." A short code is better than a long one; fewer words are better than more words.

WISDOM FROM KIDS

Lee, an experienced school-curriculum designer, shared with me a unique experience that might provide a lesson for all of us. Pre-teenagers were given a school assignment to develop a code of conduct for their class. Their first attempt resulted in a two-page listing of Dos and Don'ts - mostly Don'ts. They labored, discussed, revised, and simplified. They finally boiled their code of conduct down to three personal questions:

1) Is what I am doing helping me and others to learn?

2) Is what I am doing keeping me and others safe?

3) Is what I am doing keeping our building and the environment safe?

When the draft is brought back to the group they edit it for clarity and when all are satisfied with it, each member of the group signs the master copy. As new members later join the group they too read and sign the code, committing themselves to it.

At intervals of not more than a year, the participants review the code, perhaps slowly reading it aloud together. They consider whether in the light of experience they wish to add to or modify it.

When you first suggest working to create a code of conduct, some of the members of the group who pride themselves on being practical will probably consider that it will just be a waste of time. Usually, however, even the most skeptical members see its value when an occasion arises in the board's life that the code can help to redirect.

The examples that follow illustrate two of the many different possible approaches, each of which apparently reflects the particular history of the organization from which it came. They may assist as a starting point for a code for any board or important committee.

PINE CRESCENT RESIDENCES **Example #1**
BOARD OF DIRECTORS

CODE OF CONDUCT

We, the members of the Board of Directors of Pine Crescent Residences (PCR) commit ourselves, individually and collectively, to the following:

1) We will freely share with each other our knowledge, skills, and opinions, and to the best of our abilities act in the best interests of PCR.

2) We will treat each other with dignity and respect, which means that among other things, we will:

a) make sure that everyone who wishes has a chance to speak;

b) actively listen to each other;

c) not interrupt someone who is speaking; and

d) avoid abusive language, name calling, and questioning of others' motives.

3) We will attempt always to arrive at conclusions that we agree on collectively, but if this does not prove possible in a particular circumstance, unless we mutually agree that a minority report should be issued, each of us will accept the decision of the majority and work towards its implementation.

4) We will respect confidences entrusted to us and those that arise during our service on the board.

{Signed and dated by each board member}

SPRINGFIELD FOOD BANK **Example #2**

BOARD OF TRUSTEES

CODE OF CONDUCT

As members of the Board of Trustees we each accept the obligation to use our individual best efforts to act always in the best interests of Springfield Food Bank (SFB).

In furtherance of this solemn commitment, as a group we will:

1) When appropriate, consult with and listen to members and patrons of the SFB;

2) Inform ourselves adequately before making important decisions;

3) Respect and honor SFB's long history of balancing service and community outreach.

In our meetings and in relation to our fellow board members, as individuals we will:

1) Welcome differing views and give equal opportunity to those who express them;

2) Take only our fair turns in speaking, and encourage others to take an active part in discussion;

3) State our opinions in temperate language and acknowledge that we may not always be right.

IN WITNESS WHEREOF we have placed our respective signatures, in each others' presence.

{Signed and dated by each board member}

Appendix B

Simplified Guide To Parliamentary Procedures

THE BASICS

Parliamentary rules of order are designed to facilitate and help keep a meeting orderly, regardless of purpose. The degree to which these rules are followed precisely depends largely on the meeting size.

A meeting with a dozen or fewer participants usually proceeds more comfortably, more quickly, and more effectively if it is quite informal. Few procedural steps are needed to facilitate such small meetings and those that are desired can often be agreed upon unanimously before being framed in a motion, or even without a motion. Larger meetings and those that deal with contentious issues will be less confusing and more effective if they are conducted by following the formalities.

Precedence among authorities

There can be misunderstandings when two sources of requirements provide for different levels of compliance. For example, a governing statute may require that the notice for a meeting be sent fourteen days before the meeting, while the organization's bylaws require thirty days.

In such a situation, by complying with the longer period, the organization has also met the shorter requirement.

If, however, one source authorizes something and another source prohibits it, which is to be followed? The source higher in the following hierarchy overrules the provisions in the source that is lower. The relative rankings are, from higher to lower:

- ✓ Governing statutes;
- ✓ The organization's charter if any, and its bylaws;
- ✓ Policies and standing rules established by the organization's members in a general meeting;
- ✓ Policies and standing rules established by the organization's board;
- ✓ Meeting rules approved by those present at a meeting;
- ✓ Customs of the organization.

Quorum

- The governing statute and the organization's bylaws will usually specify, for various types of meetings, the numbers of voting members required to be present for the meeting to be valid.
- If there is no number specified for a quorum, it is a majority of the voting members.
- If at the beginning of a meeting or at any time during the meeting the number of voting members present is less than the quorum, nothing can be done during the meeting except the following:
    - recess for a stated period (during which time efforts may be made to seek a quorum);
    - set the time and date to which to adjourn the meeting; and
    - adjourn the meeting.

Main Motions--doing the business of the meeting

- A motion is a statement initiated by the words, "I move that...," which if approved will establish a policy or direct an action.
- Only one main motion can be considered at a time.
- A main motion can be amended, as long as the amendment subject matter is related to the motion.
- If an amending motion is seconded, it will be the only topic of discussion until it is approved or rejected, after which discussion on the (amended?) main motion will resume.
- A primary motion to amend can be amended by a secondary amendment, which like a primary amendment, will be the only subject of discussion until it is approved or rejected.
- A Resolution is a motion in a particular form that may begin with an explanatory preamble, headed by the word WHEREAS, and followed by the substance preceded by the words RESOLVED That...."
- Unlike the portion in the Resolved clause(s), a preamble has no legal effect.
- Most main motions should state who is to do what and when.

Approving/rejecting a motion

- In calling for the vote, the chair states the motion clearly: "It has been moved (and seconded) that..."
- Even if it appears that everyone has voted in favor of the motion, the chair asks for those opposed, using parallel wording to the request for those in favor.
- The chair does not ask for abstentions, nor take account of them.
- The chair announces the count and whether the motion has been approved or rejected.

- If there are any votes cast in favor and none cast against, the vote is unanimous.
- If it is clear that a non-contentious proposal or motion has the support of all those eligible to vote on it, the chair may declare it approved by unanimous consent (or without objection).
- A voting member can appeal, subject to a second, this (or any other) ruling by the chair.
- For most topics, a motion is approved if it receives a majority of the votes cast on it.
    - A majority is "more than half,"; that is that there are more votes in favor than those against.
    - "50% plus 1" is not the same as a majority. (When the total number of votes cast is an odd number, "50%+1" requires one more vote than a majority.)
- If a motion receives the same number of votes cast against it as have been cast for it, it has failed to receive a majority, and is rejected without any further action on it.
- A motion that rescinds or amends something that has been previously approved, or that limits a basic right of participants, usually requires a two-thirds vote, (that is that at least twice as many votes cast in favor of it as cast against it).

Closing discussion and moving forward to a vote

- No single individual can close discussion of a topic, so the chair disregards any shouts of "Question."
- To close discussion requires a motion, a second, and a vote by two-thirds of those voting on the motion.
- The motion can be "I move the previous question," or a less formal wording such as, "I move that discussion on this motion end." If the motion receives the necessary two-thirds vote in favor, all discussion must

cease immediately, and the chair proceeds to the vote on the main motion that was being discussed.

- If an amendment is pending, a vote is taken first on the amendment and then on the main motion (as amended).

APPLICATIONS FOR A SMALL MEETING

Motions and discussion

- In a small meeting, a topic can be discussed to help shape a motion before it is made.
- In all but the most simple or routine topics, the participants will better understand what is being finally considered if it is stated in the form of a motion before a vote is taken.
- A second is not necessary.
- The chair is allowed to make motions, enter discussion and vote, just as any other member, but will exercise these rights sparingly.

Procedural actions

- All of the procedural actions listed below for large meetings can be taken in a small meeting, often by informal unanimous agreement.

APPLICATIONS FOR AN AGM (or any large meeting)

Motions and discussion

- Except for perhaps a brief introduction of a topic, no discussion can take place until after a motion has been made, seconded, and stated by the chair.
- The chair takes no part in discussion of a topic and does not answer any questions or become involved

in the meeting's business except by conducting the meeting and managing parliamentary procedure.

Amending a bylaw

- Specific requirements are usually set out in the governing statute and often in the bylaws as well; all must be followed strictly.
- These provisions will specify how long before the meeting the members must be given notice of the intention to amend the bylaw.
- Usually the notice must include the exact wording of the proposed Special Resolution to make the change, although some provisions allow an explicit statement of the effects of the proposed change;
- At the meeting the proposed wording may be amended by a majority vote, but if an amendment is approved that makes a material change in the effect of the Special Resolution, it cannot be voted on at this meeting, but must be the subject of a new notice and a subsequent meeting.
- Approval of the Special Resolution requires a vote of two-thirds (in some jurisdictions, three-quarters) of those voting on it.
- In some jurisdictions, the change does not come into effect until it has been filed with the appropriate public authorities.

Nominations and elections

- Usually, a nominating committee nominates at least one eligible member for each position to be filled.
- Every voting member is entitled to nominate one or more additional eligible members for each position to be filled.
- A nomination does not require a second.
- A nomination is valid only if and when the nominee has assented to it.

- Closing nominations for a position requires a motion and a two-thirds vote.
- If there is only one nominee for a position, unless the statute or bylaws provide otherwise, the chair may be authorized to declare that person elected by acclamation, but only if there is a motion, second, and two-thirds vote to give this authorization, (because it denies the members the opportunity to make write-in votes).

Procedural steps regarding a motion that are open to discussion and that require a majority vote

✓ Adopt the agenda.

✓ Refer a motion to a committee to deal with the topic.

✓ Recess the meeting for a stated length of time.

✓ Postpone consideration of a topic to a stated time.

✓ Postpone consideration of a topic indefinitely (i.e. disposing of it without making a decision about it).

Procedural steps that are not open to discussion and that require a majority vote

✓ Adjourn the meeting.

Procedural steps regarding a motion that are open to discussion and that require a 2/3 vote

✓ Adopt standing rules for a convention.

✓ Amend agenda after it has been adopted.

✓ Amend or rescind something previously adopted.

Procedural steps regarding a motion that are not open to discussion and that require a 2/3 vote

- ✓ Close discussion of a topic (i.e. "Move Previous Question," or "Move to Close Discussion").
- ✓ Limit or extend time for discussion of a topic.
- ✓ Close nominations for a position.

Procedural steps that a single member can take

- ✓ Divide a motion that contains two or more distinct subject matters.
- ✓ Make a parliamentary inquiry (i.e. a member asks the chair for explanation of a procedure or for advice as to how to accomplish a procedural objective).
- ✓ Make a point of order (i.e. a member says that something is in violation of standing rules, of a bylaw, of a statute, etc.; the chair makes a ruling or submits the question to the assembly to decide).
- ✓ Appeal a ruling (i.e. a member says that a ruling by the chair is incorrect; after a second and limited discussion the question is put to the assembly; the ruling is sustained unless a majority of those voting on the question vote that it is incorrect).

Appendix C

Making Financial Reports Understandable

THE NEED TO TRANSFORM FINANCIAL REPORTING

The board as a whole and each board member individually are responsible ethically and legally for maintaining the organization's fiscal integrity. They can only fulfill this obligation if they understand what is happening financially within the organization from day to day. They have to know, not guess, what the organization can afford and what it cannot, and whether it will be able to keep on paying its bills. The only way they can know this is through the financial reports.

Yet, when presented with a financial report many board members' eyes glaze over, and when queried say something like, "Oh, I don't understand these reports. I figure that the treasurer will tell us if there is anything we need to know."

For their own personal protection and for that of the organization they cannot let this state of affairs remain uncorrected. The difficulty lies not with the board members but with the reports. So the reports are where we look. It helps to remember that financial reports are not ends in themselves, but are only tools in a broader financial-reporting system.

THE BASIC SYSTEM

For an organization, the appropriate accounting system is on a "cash basis." It tracks money in ("Receipts") and money out ("Disbursements"). This contrasts with the "accrual basis," which reflects commitments rather than cash flow, and includes such matters as changes in inventories. It is suitable for a business that needs to know its profit or loss each month.

Four words encapsulate a useful financial reporting system for an organization. They are:

- ✓ Control;
- ✓ Consolidate;
- ✓ Compare; and
- ✓ Comment.

Control For the financial reports to have any meaning they must include all monies that have gone in and out of the organization. The treasurer definitely does not control *how* they have been brought in, *how* they are spent, or *by whom*, but the financial records must reflect the complete story. This means, for example, that those responsible for a program or an event cannot use any of the proceeds from it to pay its costs. All receipts must be deposited intact and disbursements made in the usual manner, independent of the receipts from the event. Only in this way can the full story be reported, not only for current understanding but to help guide the budgeting process for any similar programs or events in the future.

Consolidate What puts most people off about the usual financial reports is that they seem to be entries in a contest to see how many figures can be crammed onto each page. A monthly report to the board (and similar reports to the general membership) should have only a single page of figures. Keeping it to one page requires consolidating like-items, for example, reporting all utilities as a single figure instead of separate lines for gas, water, sewer, electric power, etc. Unless there is a reason for such individual items to be reported separately, many groupings of items can be found so the readers are not overwhelmed with a mass of figures that would keep them from grasping the overall picture. While we are simplifying, let's drop pennies, so the figures that remain are able to stand out and be readily absorbed by the readers. At the same time, a more detailed, multi-page report with a line-by-line listing can be prepared. It is held in the files, and is only brought out for an auditor, or if someone requests it to follow a particular sub-budget.

Compare A raw figure means very little. It is only meaningful if it is *compared with* something. For example, if by the fifth month of the fiscal year the disbursements for travel have equaled $2,376, what does this tell anyone? Very little. It only makes sense when compared with the $3,000 that was included (for the purposes of this example) in the annual budget as the total travel costs for the year. It then says that unless travel disbursements in the remaining seven months are at a lower rate than has been the case up to now, the annual budget will be exceeded. But is there reason to panic when this budget line for travel shows that disbursements through the fifth month are greater than five-twelfths of the forecast annual total? Not necessarily. Let's suppose that the only travel expense that will be reimbursable is for the annual convention, and it occurred in the first month of the year, so there will be no more disbursements for travel. Now we can see that this line item will show a surplus of $624 at the end of the year. By knowing this at this time, the board may be able to allocate for some other purpose this money that has been freed up. The real meaning of any figure can only be found when it is compared with the amount that has been forecast to be received or disbursed in the period ending with the month in question. You can see that by including such comparisons, the figures suddenly have a meaning that allows the board and the members to make best use of the money that is and that will likely become available – with no ugly fiscal-year-end surprises.

Comment In addition to the one page of consolidated figures, there needs to be perhaps a half-page for comments by the treasurer, highlighting the overall picture and any anomalies that have appeared. The treasurer is, of course, uniquely qualified to write these comments. In the example of the hypothetical fifth month's financial report, these comments might be something like the following:

FRIENDS OF THE MUSEUM
BUDGET ANALYSIS

Five months ending with the month of ___________.2xxx

1)Travel costs for the convention have been paid, leaving an excess of $624 in this budget line that will not be needed.

2) Clerical wages and associated payroll taxes for this period have exceeded by $1,847 the forecasted budget for the first five months because it was necessary to hire some temps to help cover work until Jonathon returned from sick leave. This over-run will be met from the Contingency Fund, which is still at a satisfactory level.

3) The roof repair has been completed and paid for at the contract price, as budgeted.

4) All other individual budget lines are within range of the amounts forecasted, so the forecasted year-end balance still appears on target.

/s/ Melanie Carson, Treasurer .   Date: 08 (Month) 2xxx, .

As described in Chapter 3, the financial reports and the accompanying commentary are provided to the board members a few days before the scheduled meeting. Then, if anyone has concerns that need to be discussed, these concerns can be added to the agenda. Otherwise, by following these methods, the board members have been thoroughly informed, but without having to use precious meeting time.

Appendix D

Words You Can Use

The "Say" column of the following table suggests wordings the chair can use in various circumstances, in preference to those in the "Instead of" column (which are either uninformative or incorrect, or place an undesirable focus on the person of the chair).

INSTEAD OF--	SAY--
I'll be starting the meeting soon.	It is now (*6:58*). Please take your places so we can start on time.
I call the meeting to order. I see a quorum is present.	The meeting is called to order. A quorum is present.
Five days ago you received the draft minutes of the last meeting. Are there any corrections or additions?	Five days ago you received the draft minutes of the meeting held (*date*). Are there any corrections?
I would like a motion for this.	Is there a motion to ...?
Susan has moved that	There is a motion that ....

I need a second.	Is there a second?
We have a motion. Do you want to discuss it?	It has been moved and seconded that ....Is there discussion?
(*Ms/Mr X*) has the floor	The chair recognizes (*Ms/Mr X*).
Any objection? (*pause*). Then it's approved.	Is everyone agreed that ...? (*pause*) It is approved by unanimous consent.
Are you ready for the question?[5]	Are you ready to close this discussion and vote?
The previous question has been moved. Will those in favor It has been moved and seconded that discussion on this topic be please raise their hand. Opposed?.	closed and we move immediately to a vote. Will those in favor of doing so ...*etc.* Will those opposed to closing discussion and moving to a vote please...(*etc.*)
Will those in favor please stand?	Will those in favor of ... please stand and remain standing until the chair asks you to resume your seats.
It has a majority. Approved by 6 to 3 with 2 abstentions.	The motion is approved by a vote of 6 to 3.
Approved by 6 to 3, which is a 2/3 majority.	The motion received a vote of 6 to 3, which meets the required 2/3.
The chair has been challenged.	There has been an appeal of the ruling that ....
Are there any further nominations? Are there any further nominations?? For the third and last time, are there any further nominations?	Are there any further nominations for the position of (*treasurer*)?
I declare the meeting adjourned.	If there is no further business the meeting is adjourned
I want a motion to adjourn the meeting.	Is there a motion to adjourn this meeting?

5 Some parliamentarians still use this term. Unfortunately, often some members of a group are not familiar with it, so they do not realize that its purpose is to shut down discussion.

Afterword

Now that you have read or at least glanced through this book, you must be asking yourself, "How can I make use of this information?" Probably the best way is to run through it again, making notes or marking the margin at points that are new to you or that you especially want to remember and apply.

You might wish to spend a few minutes re-reading the segments of Chapter 1 that deal with organizational culture. These segments will relate especially to what you will be doing as you transform the board. It would also not be amiss to read Chapter 2 once again to refresh your thinking about the fundamental roles of the chair.

If you feel apprehensive about parliamentary procedure, a few minutes spent with Appendix B should alleviate your concerns.

Having done these things, you will be ready to tackle your first agenda using the new methods. Before announcing your plans for transformation of the board it would probably be useful to practice by drafting an agenda that might fit a hypothetical meeting of this board. Preparing a practice draft will help you to be ready for the real version of the agenda for your first meeting that reflects your new plans.

Then you will probably want to sit back and think about what you want to accomplish and how quickly you feel the transition can be introduced. You will decide whether you think it will be best to proceed one piece at a time or as a complete package to be presented at an orientation workshop, as described in Chapter 1.

You are now on your way to holding the best meetings you can possibly visualize, and to earning sincere (although seldom voiced) appreciation from the participants.

Enjoy the process.

Acknowledgements

This account would be incomplete if I failed to acknowledge my profound debt to our Writers' Group--Chris Bullock, May Partridge, Carolyn Redl, and Kay Stewart--professional writers all. We met monthly for the better part of three years, each sharing with the others portions of our writing in many styles and genres--all for serious critiques from the others. This book is immensely more complete, more direct, and more readable than it could have been without the benefit of the group's collective perceptions and counsel.

Heather and Marty Oppenheimer generously took on the demanding task of the pre-final copy editing. It was also their suggestion to lighten up the text with appropriate cartoons, which they helped me to find and collect.

Theo Postulo, my standby computer guru, has bailed me out countless times when I have become baffled by some cyber complexities.

Barbara Joyce Densmore has offered outstanding advice as to how best to make this book available to potential users.

Four other special people have provided support that has been invaluable throughout lifetime, including the long months of writing and editing. From their diversity of life experiences, they have helped me to broaden my perspective on meetings and to find the creativity to discover what works and the humility to concede what doesn't work. Most of all they have uniformly showered me with their love and good humor. My gratitude is boundless to (chronologically) the Rev. Eric Partridge, Dr. Brian Partridge, Sara Weicker-Partridge, and Nancy Partridge.

And, topping all of the sources of support I have been receiving, I owe appreciation beyond mere words, to my wife, Dr May Partridge. Only someone with her breadth of experience and education, lifelong skill in writing, and deep empathy, could have given me the gentle nudges when I needed them, while generously forgiving my long hours anti-socially closeted with my keyboard. Finally, as my physical health began to limit my efforts, May has valiantly helped me to shepherd the manuscript through the throes of publication and the distribution of the finished product.

To all of these wonderful, generous people, and to a legion of representatives of the publisher, I give my heartfelt appreciation. They have all been deeply involved, but any remaining errors or misconceptions are mine and mine alone.

Bruce Partridge, LL.B.(Can), J.D.(US)
Cedar, British Columbia

About The Author

Bruce Partridge is a survivor – a survivor of several thousand meetings!

Like many people who will pick up this book, Bruce has found meetings to be a vital part of his professional work life, and also of his life as a community volunteer.

During his first career he served at different times in several large Canadian and American universities in various administrative positions, including vice-president for finance and administration, executive vice president and president.

In his second career he was a corporate lawyer and then managing director of a large law firm's office in Hong Kong. In all of these positions his working day usually included at least two or three meetings with groups of all sizes, ranging from a handful of participants to an auditorium full of individuals each passionately arguing for some particular point.

Throughout these years, he also chaired or attended many meetings for various volunteer, charitable, homeowner, and religious organizations. All of them thrived on, or suffered from, how well these meetings were planned and carried out.

Some meetings were dynamic, effective and efficient. Regrettably, many of them (including a few he admits to having chaired himself early in his careers) were time-consuming, tedious, and relatively unproductive.

In this book Bruce shares what he has learned in his many years of varied experience. Using it, you can learn to plan and conduct meetings that are democratically managed , effective, and yes, enjoyable for you and for all of the participants.

Printed in Canada